Harvey Special Reports Series

Data Protection in Employment

Harvey Special Reports Series
Data Protection in Employment

by

Lovells Employment Group

Edited by

Naomi Feinstein

Susan Henderson

Lovells, Solicitors

LexisNexis™ UK

Members of the LexisNexis Group worldwide

United Kingdom	LexisNexis UK, a Division of Reed Elsevier (UK) Ltd, Halsbury House, 35 Chancery Lane, LONDON, WC2A 1EL, and 4 Hill Street, EDINBURGH EH2 3JZ
Argentina	LexisNexis Argentina, BUENOS AIRES
Australia	LexisNexis Butterworths, CHATSWOOD, New South Wales
Austria	LexisNexis Verlag ARD Orac GmbH & Co KG, VIENNA
Canada	LexisNexis Butterworths, MARKHAM, Ontario
Chile	LexisNexis Chile Ltda, SANTIAGO DE CHILE
Czech Republic	Nakladatelství Orac sro, PRAGUE
France	Editions du Juris-Classeur SA, PARIS
Germany	LexisNexis Deutschland GmbH, FRANKFURT and MUNSTER
Hong Kong	LexisNexis Butterworths, HONG KONG
Hungary	HVG-Orac, BUDAPEST
India	LexisNexis Butterworths, NEW DELHI
Ireland	LexisNexis, DUBLIN
Italy	Giuffrè Editore, MILAN
Malaysia	Malayan Law Journal Sdn Bhd, KUALA LUMPUR
New Zealand	LexisNexis Butterworths, WELLINGTON
Poland	Wydawnictwo Prawnicze LexisNexis, WARSAW
Singapore	LexisNexis Butterworths, SINGAPORE
South Africa	LexisNexis Butterworths, Durban
Switzerland	Stämpfli Verlag AG, BERNE
USA	LexisNexis, DAYTON, Ohio

© Reed Elsevier (UK) Ltd 2004
Published by LexisNexis UK

A CIP Catalogue record for this book is available from the British Library.

ISBN 0 406 97879 4

Printed and bound in Great Britain by William Clowes Limited, Beccles and London

Visit LexisNexis UK at www.lexisnexis.co.uk

Preface

It's surprising how quickly things can change. Just a few years ago data protection law was the preserve of a handful of specialists. Today, it's a hot topic. Many people are now aware that data protection is an important issue, so much so that the Data Protection Act 1998 is by far and away the most accessed piece of legislation on the HMSO website.

In fact, there can be few other recent legislative developments which have had such a pervasive impact on organisations' day-to-day working practices. This is unsurprising when you consider that two of the core principles underlying data protection law are the protection of personal privacy and the need to ensure that information held about people is accurate. One need only look at the headlines of a daily newspaper to see that privacy especially is becoming an increasingly important right in the 21st century. Our expanding capability to capture, analyse and otherwise process personal information about people raises serious risks that privacy rights are being eroded. The growing awareness of this problem over time has been reflected by the introduction of progressively more comprehensive legislation, with the DPA 1998 now at its core.

Data protection has had a lot of bad press in recent months, most notably in light of the Soham murder trial and the death of an elderly couple from the winter cold when their gas supply was cut off. In both cases the organisations involved (respectively the Humberside Police and British Gas) blamed the DPA 1998 for their failure to deal appropriately with information they had received. These claims have quite rightly been criticised by Richard Thomas, the current Information Commissioner, as an attempt to use the legislation as a 'smokescreen' for poor practice.

What these incidents do fairly highlight, however, is that the DPA 1998 can be difficult to apply in practice. Even the Information Commissioner acknowledges that it is a 'cumbersome' piece of legislation. One of his general duties is the preparation and dissemination of guidance for good practice and, given the recent furore over the DPA 1998, Richard Thomas has said that he is keen to ensure that his Office produces guidance which is both practical and user friendly.

The employment arena is one key area which the Information Commissioner has already identified as being ripe for guidance, and he is producing a four-part Employment Practices Data Protection Code of Practice. At the time of writing, three parts of the Code of Practice have been issued, the fourth part is out in draft and the Information Commissioner hopes to review and finalise the whole Code of Practice during the course of 2004 (once he has revisited parts 1 and 2). The earlier parts of the Code of Practice need quite substantial amendment to take account of the recent landmark Court of Appeal decision in *Durant v FSA* [2003] EWCA Civ 1746, which has altered our understanding of some of the most fundamental data protection concepts.

It should be remembered that the basic legal requirement on each employer is to comply with the DPA 1998 itself. Employers have to balance the various relevant issues covered by the legislation and make their own assessment of what is appropriate to their circumstances. The Code of Practice is designed to help in this regard, and sets out recommendations as to how to comply with the DPA 1998. However, the Code of Practice does not (and cannot) tell employers what is right or wrong in every case, and employers may have alternative ways of meeting the requirements of the legislation which may be both lawful and appropriate.

Data protection issues arise throughout the life cycle of the employment relationship, from recruitment through to termination of employment and beyond. This Report covers issues that employers will encounter on a regular basis, including record keeping, access requests, monitoring, data protection in the context of corporate transactions and the transfer of data overseas. Our aim is to explore these issues in detail and suggest practical solutions that employers (and their advisers) may wish to bear in mind.

The law is as at March 2004 (although we have mentioned forthcoming developments where we are aware of them). Although the DPA 1998 generally applies to the UK, other legislation referenced in this Report varies across the UK's different constituent parts. Accordingly, the law in this Report is the law of England and Wales. The situation in Scotland is very similar, but where there are material differences these have been highlighted in the text.

The production of this Report was very much a team effort by members of the Lovells employment group, with a contribution from Heather Rowe (who specialises in data protection outside the employment context). Authors are: Maya Cronly-Dillon, Helena Davies, Susan Henderson, Antonia Holmes, John Keith, Rachel Mann, Lisa Mayhew, Heather Rowe and Adam Turner. The editors are Naomi Feinstein and Susan Henderson. Many areas on which we have commented are matters of opinion – it remains to be seen if the law and practice will evolve as we have predicted!

Lovells

March 2004

Contents

Chapter 1

An overview of data protection law in the employment context 1

Helena Davies

Contents

Chapter 2

Employment records **25**

Susan Henderson

Chapter 3

Information about employees' health **37**

Rachel Mann

Chapter 4

Subject access requests **49**

Lisa Mayhew

Contents

Chapter 5

Monitoring in the workplace **67**

John Keith

Contents

Chapter 9

Miscellaneous issues 105

Adam Turner

Appendix A

The Durant case: the Information Commissioner's paper 115

Contents

Table of statutes

Table of cases

Chapter 1

An overview of data protection law in the employment context

Helena Davies

Introduction

The Data Protection Act 1998 ('the DPA 1998') governs the processing of 'personal data', that is, information about living people. It places certain obligations on 'data controllers' who are the individuals, companies or other entities who determine the purposes for which and the manner in which any personal data is processed. The DPA 1998 covers some manual records as well as computerised records and has two main effects:

- it gives individuals (known as 'data subjects') certain rights; and
- it requires data controllers to comply with data protection principles when they process personal data.

Failure to process data in accordance with the DPA 1998 can ultimately lead to a criminal offence being committed and can give rise to claims for compensation.

Employers use personal data in a variety of situations, for example:

- names, addresses and telephone numbers for telephone directories or to enable employees to be contacted in an emergency;
- bank account details, to pay salaries;
- information about family members, again for emergency contact or as next of kin;
- information about marital status for insurance purposes;
- information about health, to pay sick pay or for health and safety duties or pension scheme purposes;
- information for the purposes of equal opportunities monitoring;
- photographs, for security passes and intranet sites;
- personal details on job application forms.

Nearly all employers will be data controllers and will therefore be required to process this sort of data in accordance with the data protection principles. They may be under a duty to notify the Information Commissioner of their processing; to give data subjects access to personal data; and to have agreements with all those processing data on their behalf. They will need to address what steps to take to obtain consent to, and provide information about, the data processing they are doing and consider how to ensure this processing is properly limited and secure. In addition, there are duties *not* to disclose information to third parties which require employers to ensure staff are fully aware of their obligations. These duties are covered in detail in Chapter 2 on employment records.

Employers will find that they have to consider the balance between employees' rights and the need to run their businesses in all aspects of the human resources function from recruitment practices to administration of employment and health records, and the monitoring of employees in the workplace.

General guidance for organisations is contained in the Information Commissioner's '*Legal Guidance*'[1]. There is also specific guidance on how employers should follow the DPA 1998 in the Employment Practices Data Protection Code. This is commonly referred to as the 'Code of Practice'. The Code of Practice contains the Information Commissioner's recommendations as to how the legal requirements of the DPA 1998 can be met, although it is not the only way of achieving compliance.

This chapter outlines general data protection concepts, considering the key provisions of the DPA 1998 and underlying themes, including what information is covered, who is subject to the DPA 1998 and the eight data protection principles. In addition, the chapter explains the difficult issue of consent and the extent to which employers can rely on employees' consent as a method of compliance with their obligations under the DPA 1998. We also discuss enforcement and, lastly, some expected changes in EU law which will have a significant impact on data protection legislation and practice as we know it today.

Personal data

'Data' is defined, in DPA 1998, s 1(1), as information which:

is being processed by means of equipment operating automatically in response to instructions given for that purpose'; or 'is recorded with the intention that it should be processed by means of such equipment'; or 'is recorded as part of a relevant filing system'; or 'forms part of an accessible record.

Under DPA 1998, s 68 this extends to include health records relating to the physical or mental health or condition of an individual, made by or on behalf of a health professional in connection with the care of that individual.

'Personal data' is data which:

relate[s] to a living individual who can be identified:
(a) from [that] data; or
(b) from [that] data and other information which is in the possession of, or is likely to come into the possession of, the data controller.

The *Legal Guidance* (para 2.2.1) points out that the same set of data can relate to two or more people and be personal data about each of them.

The concept of 'possession' of data is very wide. In the Information Commissioner's view, possession does not necessarily mean that the identifying data is in the physical control of the data controller. For example, if some data processing is contracted-out, it is still in the data controller's possession.

DPA 1998, s 1(1) specifically states that 'personal data' includes any expression of opinion about an individual and any indications of the intentions of anyone in respect of that individual.

An employer who processes appraisals of employees will be creating records which contain personal data, not only in relation to the employer's opinions of those employees, but also any recorded intention to offer or decline promotion on the basis of those opinions. (This can make such records disclosable, subject to exemptions discussed later in this chapter and in Chapter 8.)

The definition of personal data is so broad that it covers most situations in an employment context where an organisation processes information about its employees. The Code of Practice gives some examples of personal data:
- an employee's salary and banking details;
- an email about an incident involving a named employee;
- a supervisor's note book containing sections on several named individuals;
- a set of completed application forms.

The Code of Practice also gives examples of information unlikely to be covered by the DPA 1998:
- information on the salary structure for the workforce where individuals are not named and are not identifiable;
- a report on recruitment where there are no details regarding individuals;
- a report on the results of 'exit interviews' where the responses are anonymised and the results cannot be traced to individuals.

The Code of Practice concludes that 'nearly all useable information held about individual workers' will be covered.

However, the Code of Practice was drafted before the Court of Appeal in *Durant v Financial Services Authority* [2003] EWCA Civ 1746, [2003] All ER (D) 124 (Dec), gave guidance on the meaning of 'personal data'. The case was brought by an individual who had complained to the Financial Services Authority ('FSA') about Barclays Bank plc and then sought access under DPA 1998, s 7 to manual files held by the FSA concerning his complaint. The Court of Appeal held that although the complaint was brought by Mr Durant, the files on the complaint were not about him and therefore were not personal data.

Although the case is about a data subject's access to information, it has important general implications. Following the Court of Appeal's judgment on 8 December 2003, the Information Commissioner issued a paper, *The 'Durant' case and its impact on the interpretation of the Data Protection Act 1998*, 2 February 2004 ('the *Durant* paper'), which is set out in Appendix A.

The general theme of *Durant* is that the DPA 1998 should be interpreted so far as possible in the light of, and to give effect to, EC Directive 95/46/EC on the protection of individuals with regard to the processing of personal data and the free movement of such data (the 'Directive'). The case quoted with approval the statement of the Court of Appeal in *Campbell v MGN* [2002] EWCA Civ 1373, [2003] QB 633, [2003] 1 All ER 224, that because the DPA 1998 has adopted the wording of the Directive, it is not appropriate to look for the precision in the use of language that is usually expected in legislation; a purposive approach to the provisions is necessary. (*Campbell* has since been appealed to the House of Lords. However, at the time of writing no decision had been handed down.)

The question in *Durant* was what was meant by data which 'relate[s] to' an individual, in DPA 1998, s 1(1). In particular, to what extent, if any, should the information have the data subject as its focus, or main focus? In deciding this issue, the Court of Appeal looked at the purpose of DPA 1998, s 7, against the background of the Council of Europe Convention for the Protection of Individuals with regard to Automatic Processing of Personal Data 1981, and the Directive. The purpose, it concluded, is to enable an individual to check whether the data controller's processing of data unlawfully infringes the individual's privacy and, if so, to take steps to protect it. It is not 'an automatic key to any information, readily accessible or not, of matters in which the individual may be named or involved'. Nor is it to assist the individual to obtain discovery of documents that may assist in litigation or complaints against third parties. It is likely in most cases, the Court of Appeal said, that only information that names or directly refers to the individual will qualify. (The Court of Appeal said that a narrow interpretation of 'personal data' goes hand in hand with the narrow meaning of 'a relevant filing system', for the same reasons. Relevant filing systems are discussed below.)

The Court of Appeal went on to explain its view of personal data in more detail. The mere fact that a document is retrievable by reference to an individual's name does not automatically make it personal data. The information must be 'biographical' and have the data subject 'as its focus or main focus', rather than some other person with whom that individual may have been involved or some transaction or event in which the individual may have had an interest. The key question is whether it is information that 'affects [the individual's] privacy, whether in his personal or family life, business or professional capacity'. The data Mr Durant was requesting did not have the necessary personal qualities; it related to his complaints not to Mr Durant himself.

Another pointer to a narrow construction of personal data, in the Court of Appeal's view, is the inclusion in DPA 1998, s 1(1) of expressions of opinion and indications or intentions in respect of the data subject. If the term had a broad construction, this wording would be unnecessary.

The *Durant* paper says that as a result of the case, the concept of privacy is central to the definition of personal data. This, the Information Commissioner suggests, means that in assessing whether information is personal data, you should take into account whether it is capable of having an adverse impact on the individual. The two key tests of whether data affects privacy are:
* is it biographical?
* is its focus the individual?

Simply because someone's name is on a document will not make it personal data unless the inclusion of the name affects that person's privacy. It will therefore be more likely to be personal data if, as well as the name, there is other information about the person. The paper gives some examples of personal data, including 'an individual's salary details', and also non-personal data, such as a name on a document or email indicating only that it has been sent or copied to that person (but there is no other information about that person); and information about the performance of an office department (it might name an individual, but the focus will be something else).

None of these examples conflict with the earlier guidance in the Code of Practice, but the paper sets out some additional indicators as to whether information is personal data.

The interpretation of the term 'personal data' by the Court of Appeal in *Durant* is incredibly restrictive and this is not fully reflected in the Information Commissioner's revised view as set out in the *Durant* paper. It is debatable how long this interpretation will last; in particular whether it will survive scrutiny in future cases, although *Durant* itself is not being appealed or referred to the European Court of Justice. Some of the arguments on construction accepted by the Court appear to be vulnerable to challenge. In particular, the two historical reasons given for a restrictive view of 'personal data' – that the inclusion of references to 'expressions of opinion' in DPA 1998, s 1(1) would otherwise be unnecessary; and the existence of a separate definition of 'sensitive personal data' – may not stand up to close analysis.

What is certain is that there will be more debate on this issue over the coming years.

Sensitive personal data

'Sensitive personal data' is a subset of 'personal data' and, under DPA 1998, s 2, covers personal information about an individual consisting of details of:
* racial or ethnic origin;
* political opinions;
* religious beliefs or other beliefs of a similar nature;
* trade union membership;
* physical or mental health or condition;
* sexual life; and
* offences or alleged offences committed by the individual, or information as to any proceedings in relation to those offences or alleged offences.

The phrase 'beliefs of a similar nature' is intended to cover only a narrow range of beliefs which are close in nature to religious beliefs. It was not intended to encompass broader 'philosophical' beliefs (Hansard, House of Commons Standing Committee D, 12 May 1998), even though this wider definition is used in the Directive and has subsequently been used in legislation outlawing discrimination on grounds of religion or belief (the Employment Equality (Religion or Belief) Regulations 2003 (SI 2003/1660)).

In an employment context, typical examples of sensitive personal data include:
* employee sickness records;
* details of an employee's racial or religious origin, obtained during ethnic monitoring;
* details of an employee's marital status, to determine to whom death-in-service benefits should be paid.

Relevant filing systems

The Data Protection Act 1984 ('DPA 1984') only applied to automatically processed information, in other words information processed by a computer. However, under the DPA 1998, the definition of 'data' was extended to cover certain manual records as well as computerised ones. Manual data which is held in a 'relevant filing system' is now covered. A relevant filing system is defined in DPA 1998, s 1(1) as:

> any set of information which is structured, either by reference to individuals or by reference to criteria relating to individuals, in such a way that specific information relating to a particular individual is readily accessible.

The definition of 'relevant filing system' caused considerable problems during the passage of the Data Protection Bill through Parliament in 1998. Originally the clause defined the test as being whether 'particular' information was readily accessible. The then Data Protection Registrar argued that this definition went further than the Government intended because it would cover, amongst other things, 'personnel files held by employers' (House of Commons Research Paper 98/48). As a result, an amendment was made to the clause; the phrase 'specific information' was used instead of 'particular information'. This, the Government believed, would exclude 'miscellaneous collections of paper about individuals, even if the collections are assembled in a file with the individual's name or other unique identifier on the front, if specific data about the individual cannot be readily extracted from that collection'. (Hansard, House of Lords, 16 March 1998, col 467).

That change clearly did not resolve the uncertainties, however. In the House of Commons Committee, George Howarth, for the Government, described the situation as 'less certain than people would wish'. He suggested that a general personnel file, containing the records of all employees, would be a 'relevant filing system' if it had an index but not if it did not and it 'might' be a relevant filing system if specific papers were flagged in some way, or if it was limited to specific information, such as health records in date order. (Hansard, House of Commons Standing Committee D, 12 May 1998.)

The *Legal Guidance* (para 2.1.1), admitting that 'it is not wholly clear how this definition translates in practical terms in all conceivable situations', offered some pointers:

- the fact that the information must be 'in a set' suggests a grouping together of information with a common theme, such as a set of information on employees, but the grouping together need not be physical; it may be dispersed over different locations within the organisation;
- it must be structured so that information about an individual is readily accessible, in other words generally accessible at any time in the day-to-day operation of the organisation;
- 'relevant filing system' is not the same as 'file'.

However, this left open the key question of whether personnel files fall within the DPA 1998. This is clearly of significance because it affects whether, as the data subjects, employees have the right to copies of the data on their personnel files.

The Information Commissioner at first took a wide view of the meaning of 'relevant filing system'. In Part 1 of the Code of Practice, a relevant filing system is said to be 'essentially any set of information about workers in which it is easy to find a piece of information about a particular worker'. The only example it is prepared to offer of manual files **not** within the definition is 'a pile of papers left in the basement'.

Subsequently the Court in *Durant* interpreted 'relevant filing system' narrowly on the basis that under the Directive the definition was intended to mean that the filing system must have a structure that applies within the file itself rather than to the total filing system. That system must give ready access to specific information. If the person looking for information has to go through the file to find the relevant information or it is kept in chronological order, it will not be a relevant filing system. The files held by the FSA in *Durant* were a variety of documents in date order. They were not significantly structured or indexed to fall within the definition.

The Court of Appeal said that the intention behind the statutory provisions is to require, as near as possible, the same standard or sophistication of accessibility to personal data in manual filing systems as to computerised records. Relevant filing systems must enable identification of relevant information with a minimum of time and cost, through clear referencing mechanisms. The Court adopted an interpretation consistent with the Directive, in particular the emphasis in Art 2(c) and recital (27) on a file structured by reference to 'specific criteria' about individuals so as to provide 'easy access' to the personal data. Recital (15) indicates that the required easy access must be on a par with that provided with a computerised system. It is not enough that a filing system leads a searcher to a file containing documents mentioning the data subject. The file to which that search leads must be structured so as to enable easy location within it, or any sub-file, of specific information about the data subject.

The Court of Appeal concluded that a relevant filing system is limited to a system:

- in which the files forming part of it are structured or referenced in such a way as clearly to indicate, at the outset of a search, whether specific information capable of amounting to personal data of an individual requesting it under DPA 1998, s 7 is held within the system and, if so, in which file or files it is held; and
- which has, as part of its own structure or referencing mechanism, a sufficiently sophisticated and detailed means of readily indicating whether and where in an individual file or files specific criteria or information about the applicant can be readily located.

The *Durant* paper expresses the Information Commissioner's view that, in relation to subject access rights, information held in manual form will only be a relevant filing system if it is structured so that the recipient of the request (the employer, generally) can:

- retrieve files in the name of the individual and those files will contain the category of personal data requested; or
- retrieve files covering topics about individuals (such as leave, sick notes, contracts) and the files are indexed or structured to allow retrieval of information about a specific individual (because the file is sub-divided in alphabetical order for example).

The paper goes on to say that where personnel files are in individuals' names, they may not qualify as relevant filing systems unless the indexing, referencing or sub-division into categories allows retrieval of data without the need to leaf through the file. It suggests applying a 'temp test' as a rule of thumb: if you employed a temp, would he or she be able to extract specific information about an individual without any particular extra knowledge?

Strangely, however, the paper concludes that, following the Durant judgment, 'very few manual files' will be covered by the DPA 1998. This does not seem to tie in with the examples it gives at the end of the paper of the types of personnel files that would be relevant filing systems, in the context of a subject access request about leave:

- a file called 'leave' divided alphabetically;
- a file called 'Mr A' sub-divided into categories, such as leave;
- a file called 'Mr A' in a system containing only records about leave;

and the one example which would not:

- a file called 'Mr A' but not sub-divided or filed otherwise than in chronological order, or sub-divided in an unhelpful way such as 'correspondence' or 'miscellaneous'.

The flowchart overleaf summarises the position post-Durant. The main change from what was generally perceived to be the consensus before Durant is the status of personnel files arranged in date order; these, it would seem, are not now to be regarded as a relevant filing system unless they are indexed or sub-divided in some other way.

It is also possible that whether or not something is a relevant filing system may now depend on the type of request being made. The logical result of following the 'temp' test outlined in the Durant paper is that if the request is for details of leave but the files are not sub-divided according to leave, then it will not be a relevant filing system for the purposes of that request, even if the files are sub-divided in some other way that enables information about, say, absence, to be retrieved.

Data subjects

Personal information about any living individual is covered by the DPA 1998. Therefore, so far as employment law is concerned, the DPA 1998 covers information that employers collect or keep about any individual who might wish to work for them, currently works for them, or has worked for them in the past. In this Report, where appropriate, the term 'employees' is used to cover all data subjects in the workplace, including:

- job applicants (successful and unsuccessful);
- former job applicants (successful and unsuccessful);
- employees, current and former;
- agency workers, current and former;
- casual workers, current and former;
- contract workers, current and former;
- volunteers and those on work experience.

The data subject need not be a UK national or resident.

The DPA 1998 gives data subjects various rights: to have a copy of information held about them; to have inaccurate data corrected; to object to processing of personal data in some circumstances; and to apply for compensation where they have suffered damage, or damage and distress, as a result of a breach of the DPA 1998. Some of these rights are discussed under the section on 'Enforcement' below; others are discussed in more detail in Chapters 2 and 4.

Responsibilities of data controllers

The DPA 1998 applies to anyone who processes personal data. One of the main changes from the

Relevant Filing Systems

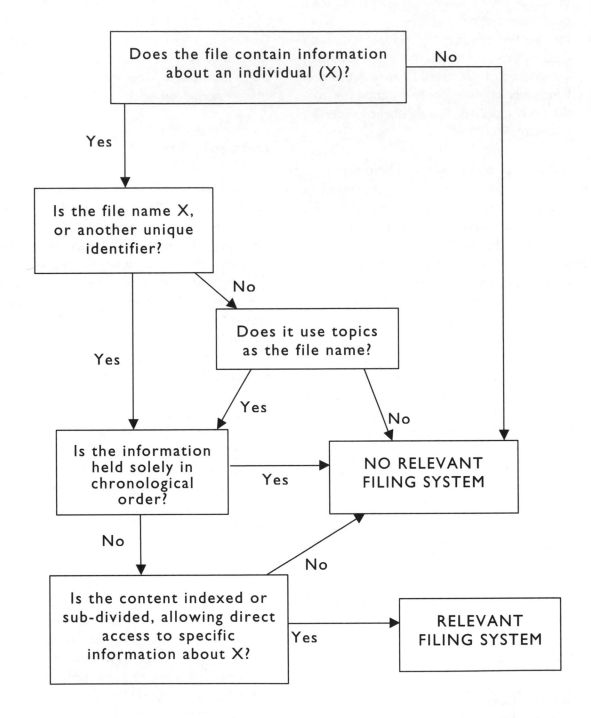

DPA 1984 is the very wide meaning of 'processing'. It includes all forms of dealing with data, including obtaining, recording, holding, organising, adapting, altering, retrieving or disclosing it. As para 2.3 of the *Legal Guidance* says, it is hard to envisage any action involving data that does not amount to processing.

Under DPA 1998, s 4(4), it is data controllers who must comply with the data protection principles. DPA 1998, s 1(1) defines data controllers as anyone who determines the purposes for which and the manner in which any personal data is processed. This can be done jointly with other data controllers; there can therefore be multiple data controllers in one organisation. For example, it is quite common for a number of companies to have access to a centralised group HR database.

In an employment context, employers are clearly data controllers, but others who process information about individuals (such as employment agencies or trade unions) may also be data controllers.

Often employers will allocate data protection responsibility to an individual or department, but this does not transfer legal liability onto individual employees or make them data controllers. Likewise, delegation to data processors (see below) does not remove the obligation on the data controllers to comply with the DPA 1998 themselves.

Data processors

Anyone who is not a data controller but who processes data on behalf of the data controller (except if they are an employee of the data controller) is known as a 'data processor'. In the employment field, if a human resources or payroll function is outsourced to a third party, that person would be a data processor. Third parties to whom administrative or other functions have been delegated may also fall within the definition of 'data controller' if they have control or discretion over the purpose and manner of processing data. It is important for employers to establish whether the third parties concerned are data controllers or data processors, because if data processors are appointed

the employer will remain responsible for complying with the DPA 1998 in respect of that data.

The DPA 1998 requires data controllers to impose certain security requirements on data processors by contract. In particular, DPA 1998, Sch 1, Part II, paras 11 and 12 require employers who use data processors to process data to choose data processors who provide sufficient guarantees as to the technical and organisational security measures that are in place in relation to that processing and also to take reasonable steps to ensure that those security measures are observed. In addition, there must be a written contract with the data processor. The contract must specify that the data processor will not accept instructions in relation to the data from anyone other than the employer, and that the data processor will take security measures sufficient to comply with the seventh data protection principle (see below).

Notification

Most data controllers will need to notify the Information Commissioner of their processing of personal data. Notification is the process by which data controllers inform the Information Commissioner of certain details about the processing of personal data they carry out. These details are then included on a public register. Data controllers or employees can inspect this register at any time by visiting the Data Protection Register website (www.informationcommissioner.gov.uk). There are some exemptions from the requirement to notify, but these are likely to apply to smaller businesses that have relatively simple data processing operations. All data controllers are required to comply with the data protection principles even where they are exempt from the requirement to notify.

Guidance on notification is contained in the Information Commissioner's *Notification Handbook* (*Notification Handbook – A Complete Guide to Notification*, available on the website (www.informationcommissioner.gov.uk) under 'Data Protection': 'Notification'). Notification can be done online.

Notification is covered in more detail in the employment records chapter.

Data protection principles

There are eight data protection principles that are central to the DPA 1998 and govern the way in which personal data can be collected and used. The principles, set out in Part I of DPA 1998, Sch I, are:

1st **fair and lawful processing**: personal data must be processed fairly and lawfully and must not be processed unless one of a number of conditions in DPA 1998, Sch 2 is met, and, for sensitive personal data, one of a more stringent set of conditions in DPA 1998, Sch 3 is also met

2nd **limited purposes**: personal data must be obtained only for specified and lawful purposes and must not be processed in a way that is incompatible with those purposes

3rd **scope**: personal data must be adequate, relevant and not excessive in relation to the purpose of the processing

4th **accuracy**: personal data must be accurate and, where necessary, kept up to date

5th **retention**: personal data must not be kept for longer than is necessary

6th **data subjects**: personal data must be processed in line with the rights of data subjects

7th **security**: appropriate technical and organisational measures must be taken against accidental loss or damage to or disclosure of personal data

8th **transfers**: except under specified conditions, personal data must not be transferred to countries outside the EEA that do not adequately protect the rights and freedoms of data subjects.

These principles are broadly similar to those in the DPA 1984, but with much more detail and, consequently, more onerous responsibilities on employers as data controllers.

The most important principle for employers is the first principle. This is discussed in detail below and summarised in the flowchart later in this chapter. The other seven principles are covered in detail in chapters on employment records and the transfer of data overseas. Brief summaries of them follow.

The first principle

To establish lawful processing under the first data protection principle:
- where 'personal data' is involved, one of the DPA 1998, Sch 2 conditions must be satisfied (see below); and
- where 'sensitive personal data' is involved, one of the DPA 1998, Sch 3 conditions must also be satisfied (see below).

In addition, the processing must be 'fair' in accordance with paras I to 4 of Part II of DPA 1998, Sch I, known as the 'fair processing code'. Compliance with the fair processing code does not guarantee fair processing, but will indicate that processing has been done fairly unless there is evidence to the contrary.

In assessing fairness, the paramount consideration is the consequences for the data subject (*Legal Guidance* para 3.1.7). Relevant factors in deciding if data has been processed fairly include:
- the method by which data is obtained. Clearly, unlawful methods of obtaining data will render the processing unfair. Personal data is deemed to have been obtained fairly if supplied to the employer by someone who is authorised or required by law to do so (DPA 1998, Sch I, Part II para 1(2));
- the information is made available by the employer to the employee. Personal data will not be treated as having been processed fairly unless the employer ensures, as far as practicable, that the employee is provided with certain information or it is made 'readily available' to the employee. The necessary information is:
  o the employer's identity or, if the employer has nominated a representative for data protection purposes, that representative's identity
  o the purpose of the processing
  o any other information 'necessary' in the 'specific circumstances' to enable the processing to be fair (DPA 1998, Sch I, Part II, para 3).

'Readily available' means that the employer can provide the information via an intranet site or notice board, rather than giving the information to each employee individually.

The *Legal Guidance* (para 3.1.7.3) notes that the more unforeseen the consequences of the processing, the more information the employer should provide. In the context of the DPA 1984, the Data Protection Tribunal has found that personal information is not fairly obtained unless the individual has been informed of the non-obvious purposes for which it is required, before the information is obtained: *Innovations (Mail Order) Ltd v Data Protection Registrar* (September 1993, unreported).

An example in an employment context that illustrates the difference between obvious and non-obvious purposes is in relation to payroll details supplied by employees. Clearly these are used to pay employees, but employees might not be aware that these details would be passed to prospective purchasers on a sale of a part or all of the company's business. This possibility should, therefore, be included in the information given to employees about processing.

There is an exception to the requirement to supply information: the employer is not obliged to do so where it has received the data from someone other than the employee and:

- to provide the information would require a disproportionate effort, or
- the processing is necessary to comply with a statutory obligation on the employer (DPA 1998, Sch I, Part II, para 3).

However, this exception is itself subject to further conditions, set out in the Data Protection (Conditions under Paragraph 3 of Part II of Schedule 1) Order 2000 (SI 2000/185). In short, the employer must provide the information if requested. And, where the 'disproportionate effort' ground is relied on, the organisation must keep a record of the reasons why it believes it does not need to provide the information. (The concept of 'disproportionate effort' is also relevant to subject access requests and is discussed in detail in Chapter 4.)

There is no definition of 'lawful' processing in the DPA 1998, but the *Legal Guidance* (para 3.1.4) suggests the areas of law of particular relevance here, especially in the public sector, are:

- confidentiality between data controller and subject;
- the rules requiring organisations to act only within the limits of their legal powers;
- legitimate expectation of the individual as to how the data controller will use the information; and
- Article 8 of the European Convention on Human Rights (the right to respect for private and family life).

The *Legal Guidance* (para 3.1.7.7) suggests that as the DPA 1998 makes no specific provision relating to timescale, the presumption must be that information to satisfy the fair processing requirement must be given to the data subject at the time the data is obtained (except in cases where the information has come from someone other than the data subject; here the *Legal Guidance* suggests a slighter more lenient timescale, but the information must be provided within a 'reasonable period of time').

The first principle has led to the common practice of the issue of a data protection policy and 'purpose statement' to all employees. This is discussed in more detail in the next chapter.

Employers should continually monitor compliance with the first principle. If it becomes clear that they hold data that they should not (because, for example, they have been given more information than they need) then it would seem that the only safe way of remedying possible breaches of the DPA 1998 would be to destroy it.

The second principle

Personal data shall be obtained only for one or more specified and lawful purposes, and shall not be further processed in any manner incompatible with that purpose or those purposes.

Data must not be processed in any manner which is incompatible with 'specified' purposes. Under DPA 1998, Sch I, Part II, para 5, the employer can specify those purposes, in the notice to employees required under the first principle, or in its notification to the Information Commissioner.

Under the DPA 1984, the second principle merely required data to be held only for specified and lawful purposes, and went on to say that it would be treated as held for a specified purpose if that purpose was described in the registration (now called notification). In effect, therefore, compliance with this principle could be established simply by notification. This is not the case under the DPA 1998 because of the additional requirement to process in a compatible manner.

The third principle

> Personal data shall be adequate, relevant and not excessive in relation to the purpose or purposes for which [it is] processed.

The terms 'adequate', 'relevant' and 'excessive' are not defined, so whether this principle is complied with will depend on the circumstances. In the context of the DPA 1984 the Data Protection Tribunal held, in *Runnymede Borough Council CCRO v Data Protection Registrar* [1990] RVR 236, that where a data controller holds an item of information on a number of individuals which will be used or useful only in relation to some of them, the information is likely to be excessive and irrelevant in relation to those individuals in respect of whom it will not be used or useful and should not be held in those cases.

The *Legal Guidance* (para 3.3) states that it is not acceptable to hold information on the basis that it might possibly be useful in the future without a view of how it will be used. It does go on to say that this is different from holding information in the case of a particular foreseeable contingency which may never occur, such as employers holding details of blood groups of employees in hazardous occupations.

Employers should not keep excessive or irrelevant records about employees. They should not, for example, collect data on the basis that it may be needed at some stage but with no clear idea of how and when. They should avoid holding the same personal data for all employees if it is in fact required only for some employees. Where circumstances change, for example remuneration packages are amended, data previously held may become redundant. If so, employers should consider deleting or destroying it.

The fourth principle

> Personal data shall be accurate and, where necessary, kept up to date.

Although it can be difficult for employers themselves to keep data up to date, it is not sufficient to rely on the fact that the information has been supplied by the employee or a third party. However, this principle will not be infringed if the employer received inaccurate personal data from the employee or a third party *and* the data accurately records the information obtained; *and* the employer took reasonable steps to ensure the accuracy of the data; *and*, if the employee has told the employer that the data is inaccurate, the data records this (DPA 1998, Sch I, Part II, para 7).

The reference to updating being required 'where necessary' means that the purpose for which data is held is relevant to deciding whether updating is required. For example, for data which is essentially a historical record, updating is inappropriate. On the other hand, data used to decide whether to confer or withhold a benefit should clearly be kept up to date.

This principle is discussed in detail in Chapter 2.

The fifth principle

> Personal data processed for any purpose or purposes shall not be kept longer than is necessary for that purpose or purposes.

There is a fine line to be drawn between destroying out-of-date or redundant data, and keeping data that may be required for proper administration or where legal issues could arise. There is also other legislation on retention of certain categories of data which needs to be factored in; such as the Police and Criminal Evidence Act 1984 and the Information Commissioner's CCTV Code of Practice. This is also discussed in detail in the chapter on employment records.

The sixth principle

> Personal data shall be processed in accordance with the rights of data subjects under the DPA 1998.

DPA 1998, Sch 1, Part II, para 8 limits contravention of this principle to certain situations:

- the employer fails to give an employee information to which the employee is entitled under DPA 1998, s 7 (the subject access rights);
- the employer fails to comply with a request under DPA 1998, s 10 not to process personal data on the grounds that it will cause damage and distress (see 'Enforcement' below);
- the employer fails to comply with a notice under DPA 1998, s 11 not to process data for the purposes of direct marketing; or
- the employer fails to comply with a request under DPA 1998, s 12 to ensure that certain categories of decisions about the employee are not made completely automatically (see Chapter 9).

The seventh principle

> Appropriate technical and organisational measures shall be taken against unauthorised or unlawful processing of personal data and against accidental loss or destruction of, or damage to, personal data.

This deals with security of data and is covered in detail in the chapter on employment records.

The eighth principle

> Personal data shall not be transferred to a country or territory outside the EEA unless that country or territory ensures an adequate level of protection for the rights and freedoms of data subjects in relation to the processing of personal data.

This is dealt with in Chapter 7.

DPA 1998, Sch 2 conditions

DPA 1998, Sch 2 conditions, one of which must be satisfied for the processing of personal data are:

- **the individual has given his consent to the processing** (this is discussed below under 'Consent');
- **the processing is necessary for the performance of a contract with the employee or for taking steps at the request of the employee with a view to entering into a contract.** Examples of this condition are where an employer processes information to run its payroll in order to pay its employees; processing of job applications; and processing mortgage references for employees. However, this would not extend to processing that may benefit the employer, but which it is not strictly obliged to do (such as email or internet monitoring);
- **the processing is necessary for compliance with any non-contractual legal obligation to which the employer is subject.** For example, monitoring the number of hours worked by an employee to ensure compliance with the Working Time Regulations 1998 (SI 1998/1833), or the National Minimum Wage Act 1998, or in order to comply with income tax withholding obligations;
- **the processing is necessary to protect the vital interests of the employee for example, to disclose an employee's medical history in the case of an emergency.** The *Legal Guidance* (para 3.1.1) says this can only be relied on where the processing is necessary for matters of life and death;

- the processing is necessary for the administration of justice or the exercise of functions of government departments or other statutory functions. This may be relevant to public sector bodies;

- **the processing is necessary for the purposes of 'legitimate interests' pursued by the employer or by third parties to whom data is disclosed, except where the processing is unwarranted because it prejudices the rights and freedoms or legitimate interests of the data subject.** An example which might satisfy this condition would be where the employer transfers due diligence employee data to a third party for the purposes of selling the business (see Chapter 6).

According to the *Legal Guidance,* the Information Commissioner takes a wide view of the legitimate interest condition. In para 3.1.1 it recommends that two tests should be applied to:

- establish the legitimacy of the data controller's interests; and

- ascertain whether the processing is unwarranted by reason of prejudice to the rights of the data subject.

> Although much processing carried on by employers is within the 'legitimate interest' condition, as it could be said to be necessary for the operation of human resources management, the scope of this condition has never been clear and, as a result, many employers have attempted to rely on getting consent. For reasons which are discussed below, under 'Consent', this may not be best practice.

Many of the DPA 1998, Schs 2 and 3 conditions stipulate that the processing must be 'necessary' for the purpose set out in the particular condition. The Information Commissioner's view (para 3.1.1 of the *Legal Guidance*) is that in determining whether or not something is 'necessary' data controllers should consider objectively whether:

- the purposes of processing are valid;
- they can only be achieved by the processing; and
- the processing is proportionate to the aim.

DPA 1998, Sch 3 conditions

Where 'sensitive personal data' is involved, an employer must comply not just with at least one DPA 1998, Sch 2 condition, but also with at least one DPA 1998, Sch 3 condition. DPA 1998, Sch 3 conditions are harder to satisfy than DPA 1998, Sch 2 conditions. This reflects the fact that sensitive personal data by definition deals with more private matters than ordinary personal data. DPA 1998, Sch 3 conditions that may apply in an employment context include:

- **the employee has given his explicit consent to the processing of data.** This issue is discussed below in the section on 'Consent';

- **the processing is necessary for the purposes of exercising or performing any right or obligation imposed by law on the employer in connection with employment**

The Code of Practice notes that this condition can have quite wide application. Employers have many obligations under statute or common law (decisions in legal cases), for example to ensure health and safety at work; prevent discrimination; check the immigration status of employees; and they have financial responsibilities and duties under the DPA 1998 itself. Therefore, employers may be able to collect information on matters such as employees' criminal records or health if it is necessary to enable employers to meet their legal obligations. But Part 1 of the Code of Practice notes that the requirement that the collection of data must be 'necessary' means that, for example, employers should not collect information on the criminal convictions of *all* job applicants if the duty to protect staff and customers can be secured by obtaining information only on successful applicants or particular categories of successful applicants.

Part 2 of the Code of Practice says that this condition covers maintaining statutory sick pay and maternity pay records or company sick pay records (where the employment contract provides for it); and (perhaps surprisingly) that the condition could be relied on to enable an employer to keep sickness records more generally on the basis that this is necessary to ensure the employer does not dismiss unfairly.

Part 3 of the Code of Practice, on monitoring at work, says the condition would be satisfied if there were evidence that an employee was using the employer's email to subject another employee to harassment, and there was no reasonable alternative to monitoring (see further Chapter 5 on monitoring);

- **the processing is necessary for the protection of the employee's vital interests where the employee cannot give consent; for example, in life and death emergencies;**
- **the processing is carried out in the course of its legitimate activities by a non-profit making political, philosophical, religious or trade union body and relates only to individuals who are members of or have regular contact with the body, and there are safeguards for data subjects' rights and freedoms;**
- **the information has deliberately been made public by the employee;**
- **the processing is necessary in connection with any legal proceedings or for the purposes of obtaining legal advice.** Part 1 of the Code of Practice notes that this might be relied on where an employer needs to process sensitive personal data for the purpose of defending employment litigation;
- **the processing is necessary for the administration of justice (see DPA 1998, Sch 2);**
- **the processing is necessary for medical purposes and was undertaken by a health professional or someone else subject to an equivalent duty of confidentiality;** for example, where a company doctor treats an employee;
- **data on racial or ethnic origin is processed for equal opportunities monitoring purposes.** This is extended by an Order (see below) to other types of monitoring (religious beliefs and disability). Processing must be 'necessary', so Part 1 of the Code of Practice recommends that wherever practicable monitoring should be based on anonymous information;
- **data is processed under the Data Protection (Processing of Sensitive Personal Data) Order 2000 (SI 2000/417).** This covers certain very specific instances of processing, such as where it needs to be carried out without explicit consent

(for example to prevent or detect crime); certain disclosures for journalistic, artistic or literary purposes; confidential counselling functions; certain insurance or pension scheme contexts; and limited processing by political parties or for research purposes.

Consent

One of the DPA 1998, Sch 2 conditions is that the individual has given consent to the processing. Although all conditions provide an equally valid basis for processing, employers have, naturally, tended to look to the consent condition because it appears to provide a clear cut way of complying – you either have consent or you do not, it might be thought. However, it is not as simple as this. 'Consent' is not defined by the DPA 1998. Article 2(h) of the Directive defines it as:

> any freely given specific and informed indication of his wishes by which the data subject signifies his agreement to personal data relating to him being processed.

It also refers later to the data subject 'unambiguously' giving consent (Art 7(a)). The *Legal Guidance* specifically approves of the Directive's definition.

In Parliament the (then) Solicitor-General indicated that consent could be given in a general way, via a standard contractual clause or box to tick, for matters such as insurance applications, but that different considerations would apply to employees whose contracts purported to contain consent clauses. He concluded that it would be for courts to decide whether or not consent had been properly given (Hansard House of Lords, 2 February 1998, col 478; 23 February 1998, col CWH 15-16; Hansard House of Commons Standing Committee D 4 June 1998).

The *Legal Guidance* states the Information Commissioner's view that consent is not particularly easy to achieve and that data controllers should consider other conditions in DPA 1998, Sch 2 (and DPA 1998, Sch 3, if processing sensitive personal data) before looking at consent. The *Legal Guidance* notes that the fact that the data subject must 'signify'

Data processing under the first principle

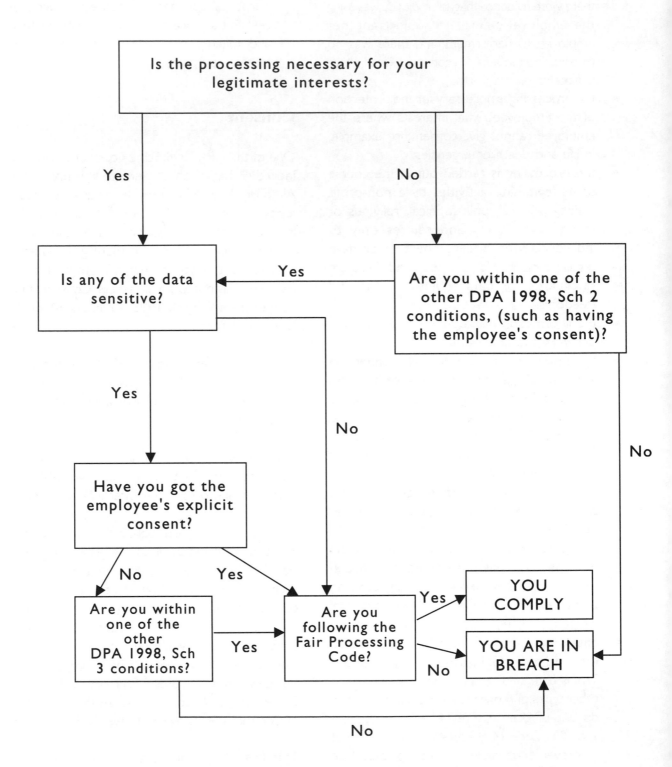

his agreement means that there must be some active communication between the parties, although a data subject may signify agreement other than in writing. Data controllers can certainly not infer consent from non-response to a communication. Clearly consent obtained under duress or on the basis of misleading information will not be valid. In addition, as consent must be 'informed', this means that the employee must know and understand what he is agreeing to.

The Information Commissioner's *Guide to the Practical Implementation of the Data Protection Act 1998* (available on the website www.information commissioner.gov.uk) (not tailored specifically to employers) suggests a number of considerations to be taken into account in deciding if valid consent has been given:

- the explanation of processing is clearly expressed, not 'buried in the small print';
- there must have been some active communication (whether written or oral); consent cannot be inferred from lack of response to communication;
- there must be no element of duress or misinformation;
- although consent will normally endure for as long as the data is processed, it need not necessarily do so; sometimes data subjects may be able to withdraw consent;
- if consent is intended to endure indefinitely, this should be made clear;
- if personal data is obtained from data subjects and the required information to make the processing fair has been provided, it is likely to be valid consent.

Confusingly, the Code of Practice only discusses consent in detail in the context of sensitive personal data and 'explicit consent' (see below). It does not go through the DPA 1998, Sch 2 conditions. There are passing references to 'ordinary' consent, however, which may trouble employers. For example, in the 'Frequently Asked Questions' section of Part 1 of the Code of Practice, in answer to the question 'Do I have to get a person's consent to hold records about him or her?', the Code of Practice says: 'Consent to hold personal data relating to workers is not usually required. Indeed, the Information Commissioner considers it misleading to seek consent from workers if they have no real choice.' Part 2, on Employment Records, answers the same question in more detail, saying that an employer can 'usually' rely on the legitimate interest condition.

In the absence of clear guidance on the meaning of 'consent' the following common law principles should be considered:

- Consent can be express or implied from actions, but not inaction or silence (for example, a policy in a handbook).
- You cannot consent to something of which you have no knowledge (for example, covert monitoring).
- You cannot consent to something if you are incapable of understanding the action to which you are consenting or the nature of the contract (for example, consider employees with learning difficulties – would they be able to consent to biometric testing?)
- A fundamental mistake in relation to the contract will render any purported consent a nullity.
- An agreement may not be binding if you are induced to sign something which is fundamentally different in character to that which you contemplated.
- Undue influence may render apparent consent a nullity.
- Consent obtained by coercion or duress is not true consent – consent on which the offer of employment is dependent may not amount to consent at all.
- Reluctant consent may be valid as long as it is voluntary.
- Consent is only valid if the individual has legal capacity to consent.

Explicit consent

There appears to be less pressure on employers not to use consent as a DPA 1998, Sch 3 condition. But again, there is no definition in the DPA 1998 or the Directive of 'explicit consent'. According to the *Legal Guidance*, the fact that the DPA 1998 requires explicit consent 'to the processing of the personal data' suggests that the consent should be 'absolutely clear'. In appropriate cases it should cover the specific detail of the processing, the particular type of data to be processed (or even the specific information), the purposes of the processing and any special aspects of the processing which may affect the individual, for example disclosures which may be made of the data.

Part 1 of the Code of Practice says that where the employer is relying on explicit consent in relation to applications for employment, the applicant must have been told clearly what personal data is involved and the use that will be made of it. The applicant must have given a positive indication of agreement, such as a signature. The consent must be freely given. This means 'the applicant must have a real choice whether or not to consent and there must be no significant detriment that arises from not consenting'. Part 1 notes that in relation to recruitment this is less of an issue because the individual will have a choice as to whether or not to apply and take the job. If consent to processing of sensitive data is a condition of a job application being considered, this does not prevent the consent being freely given. As recruitment proceeds, however, it is less likely that valid consent can be obtained. If the direct consequence of not consenting is withdrawal of a job offer the consent is unlikely to be freely given. Part 2 of the Code of Practice reiterates this: if the direct consequence of not consenting is dismissal, being passed over for promotion, or the denial of a significant benefit that would be given to a consenting employee, consent is unlikely to be deemed to be freely given.

Employers seem to be in a no-win situation. The Information Commissioner has interpreted consent in such a way as to make it almost impossible to obtain. This interpretation relies on European guidance, but arguably it goes further than the wording of DPA 1998, Sch 3.

One way for employers to get employees' consent to the processing of personal data is to include a term in the contract of employment to be signed by the employee. However, this is not best practice and other methods are likely to be more appropriate.

Alternatively, processing statements can be issued to employees, explaining in detail the processing that the particular employer considers it is authorised to do (because, for example, it is covered by the 'legitimate interest' exemption) without employees' consent, and also processing which goes beyond this, or relates to sensitive personal data, and therefore requires consent. Employees are asked to sign to acknowledge their agreement to the processing. An example is included in Appendix B.

The concept of 'freely given' consent may give rise to practical difficulties. Clearly, veiled threats to employees that failure to give consent will result in withholding of pay or other benefits would not be lawful. However, it ought to be legitimate for employers to explain that, if consent is not given, the DPA 1998 will (in the vast majority of cases) still permit them to process personal data and sensitive personal data but that it may mean that (for example) they will not be able to pay company sick pay (as opposed to statutory sick pay) to an employee off sick.

Processing of sensitive personal data will definitely occur in the context of ill-health benefits and a statement giving explicit consent should be included in the paperwork at the start of any such process.

Exemptions

There are a number of exemptions from, and modifications to, various provisions of the DPA 1998. These are contained in DPA 1998, ss 28 to 38 and Sch 7. Most of them are not of direct relevance in the employment context although they may have a bearing on employers' actions. However, some have direct impact on employers.

For example, under DPA 1998, Sch 7, para 1, employment references supplied in confidence are exempt from the data subject right of access (see Chapter 4). There is also an exemption from both subject access and the provision of information requirements of the first principle for personal data processed for the purpose of management forecasting or planning, such as in connection with proposed redundancies (para 5), records of the data controller's intentions in negotiations between employer and employee (para 7) and legal professional privilege (para 10). All these are discussed in more detail in Chapter 4.

The exemptions are set out in more detail in Chapter 8.

Transitional arrangements

The transitional arrangements under the DPA 1998 centre around 'eligible data'; that is, data that is subject to processing which was already underway immediately before 24 October 1998 (DPA 1998, Sch 8, para 1(1)).

First transitional period: 24 October 1998 to 23 October 2001

During the first transitional period 'eligible manual data' was exempt from the data protection principles, the rights of employees under Part II of the DPA 1998, and the notification provisions (DPA 1998, Sch 8, para 2).

The transitional rules for manual health records were slightly different.

Processing of eligible automated data was exempt from some of the requirements of the DPA 1998. In effect, processing of eligible automated data was exempt from any of the provisions of the DPA 1998 which were not in the DPA 1984. In addition, the processing of eligible automated data for calculating employees' pay and pension entitlement was also exempt to a limited extent, provided the data was processed only for that purpose.

Second transitional period: 24 October 2001 to 23 October 2007

Eligible manual data held immediately before 24 October 1998 and manual health records not forming part of a relevant filing system have the benefit of the second transitional period (DPA 1998, Sch 8, para 14).

They are exempt from:
- the first principle, except to the extent it requires compliance with para 2 of the fair processing code (the provision of information);
- the second, third, fourth and fifth principles; and
- an employee's right to go to court for an order under DPA 1998, s 14 relating to inaccurate data.

Territorial application of the DPA 1998

DPA 1998, s 5(1) says:

> Except as otherwise provided by or under section 54, this Act applies to a data controller in respect of any data only if -
> (a) the data controller is established in the UK and the data [is] processed in the context of that establishment, or
> (b) the data controller is established neither in the UK nor in any other EEA State but uses equipment in the UK for processing the data otherwise than for the purposes of transit through the UK.

DPA 1998, s 5(3) sets out the meaning of a UK establishment, which is:

> (a) an individual who is ordinarily resident in the UK;
> (b) a body incorporated under the law of, or any part of, the UK;
> (c) a partnership or other unincorporated association formed under the law of any part of the UK; and
> (d) any person who does not fall within paragraph (a), (b) or (c) but maintains in the UK -
>   (i) an office, branch or agency through which he carries on any activity, or
>   (ii) a regular practice;
> and the reference to establishment in any other EEA State has a corresponding meaning.

Therefore, it is clear that a UK-based employer which controls the manner and purposes for which information about employees is held, will fall fairly and squarely within the remit of the DPA 1998. It is equally clear that information which is held by an overseas employer (for example an American-based company) for the purposes of that overseas company will not fall within the jurisdiction of the DPA 1998 provided its data is not processed substantively on equipment in the UK. Where it becomes more difficult is in the context of an international company where employee information is shared across the globe. This issue is best illustrated with a number of examples:

Example: Two employees, one of whom ('A') is based in London and the other of whom ('B') is based in Tokyo, each send emails to colleagues about another of their colleagues ('C') who is also based in London. C serves an access request asking to see copies of certain emails, which he believes are held in A's and B's email accounts. A's emails are searchable under the DPA 1998, as the manner and purpose for which A transmits emails is controlled by the UK entity which employs him and where he is based. However, assuming B's emails are processed through a Japanese server, his email account falls outside the jurisdiction of the DPA 1998 and is not subject accessible.

Example: The situation becomes more complex if B travels to the UK on a regular basis as part of his job. When he comes to the UK, he can log on to a PC connected to the London email servers and the technology allows him to gain access to his local email account held in Japan, so enabling him to receive and send emails as though he were still based in Japan. Does the fact that he can access his emails in Japan from London mean that his local email account is now subject accessible under the DPA 1998? The answer to this is likely to be fact-sensitive. If all B is doing is gaining access to his emails held on a Japanese email server, than the answer must be no. If, however, in gaining access, something extra happens, such as his emails are downloaded, copied and then stored in the London server, then this may constitute 'processing' within the context of the UK establishment and so is arguably caught by the DPA 1998.

An interesting aspect of the DPA 1998, s 5 is that there is no requirement for the employee (as opposed to the employer) to be established in the UK. Therefore, it would appear that a UK company which employs overseas nationals in a UK office is under the same obligations to those overseas employees with regard to data protection as it would be to its UK workforce.

Enforcement

Any enforcement action would be based on a failure to meet the requirements of the DPA 1998 itself. However, as the Code of Practice itself makes clear, relevant benchmarks in the Code of Practice would be cited by the Information Commissioner in connection with any enforcement actions relating to the processing of personal data in employment and disregard of them is likely to mean that an employer will be found not to comply with the DPA 1998.

Compliance with the DPA 1998 is regulated by the Information Commissioner who is an independent officer appointed by the Government.

Assessment; enforcement notices and offences

Under DPA 1998, s 42, an employee can ask the Information Commissioner to assess whether the employer's processing is in compliance with the DPA 1998. On receiving such a request the Information Commissioner is obliged, under DPA 1998, s 42(2), to make an assessment, unless the Information Commissioner has not been supplied with the information he reasonably requires to be satisfied as to the identity of the person making the request and of the processing in question. The Information Commissioner can serve an Information Notice on a data controller to obtain information (DPA 1998, s 43). The Information Commissioner can also serve an enforcement notice under DPA 1998, s 40, requiring changes to be brought about within an organisation to ensure compliance with the DPA 1998; for example, the deletion of records or the redesigning of an application form. Breach of the enforcement notice is a criminal offence under DPA 1998, s 47.

The employer can appeal against the enforcement notice to the independent Information Tribunal and from there to higher courts on a point of law (DPA 1998, ss 48 and 49). However, if the Tribunal upholds the enforcement notice and the employer continues to be in breach this remains a criminal offence (DPA 1998, s 47), unless the employer can prove it exercised 'all due diligence' to comply with the notice.

Other criminal offences under the DPA 1998 include:
* failure to notify where not exempt;
* failure to keep a notification up to date;
* unlawfully obtaining personal data;
* unlawfully selling data.

Where an offence has been committed by a company and with the consent or connivance of, or attributable to neglect by, a company director or other senior management, they (as well as the company) can be prosecuted (DPA 1998, s 61).

DPA 1998, s 55 makes it an offence for an employee (or anyone else) to knowingly or recklessly, without the consent of the employer:
* obtain or disclose personal data; or
* procure the disclosure of personal data to another person.

There is an exemption if the employee can show that his action was necessary to prevent or detect a crime; or if it was legally required or authorised or the employee acted in the reasonable belief that he had the legal right to take that action; or that the employer would have consented if it had known; or the action was justified in the public interest.

An individual can, either as well as or instead of complaining to the Information Commissioner, bring a claim in the courts. The claim would usually be for a declaration that there has been a failure to comply with the DPA 1998 but could also be for compensation (see below).

Enforcement of the DPA 1998 whether by the Information Commissioner or the courts is discretionary.

Fines

For offences under the DPA 1998 the sanction is a fine up to £5,000 on summary conviction and an unlimited fine on conviction on indictment (DPA 1998, s 60).

Compensation

An employee who has suffered damage as a result of a breach of the DPA 1998 can be awarded a payment of compensation from the data controller for that damage and for any distress caused (DPA 1998, s 13). Damages for distress are only available if the employee also suffers damage (meaning essentially financial loss). In any legal action for compensation, it is a defence for the employer to prove it took such care as was reasonably required (in all the circumstances) to comply with the legislation.

Actions against inaccurate data

An employee has the right under DPA 1998, s 14(1) to apply to court on the grounds that personal data relating to him is inaccurate. If the complaint is upheld, the court can order the employer to rectify, block, erase or destroy that data (or any other personal data that contains an expression of opinion based on the inaccurate data). The employer can also be ordered to notify third parties that inaccurate data has been corrected. An example of a (failed) attempt to obtain corrective action is the decision in *PUK v Wozencroft* [2002] EWHC 1724 (Fam). For more detail see Chapter 4 on subject access requests.

Where the inaccurate data is based on information received from the employee or a third party, instead of making an order under DPA 1998, s 14(1) the court may order a statement of the inaccuracy to be added to the data, provided the employer has complied with the requirements of DPA 1998, Sch 1, Part II, para 7, by taking reasonable steps to check the accuracy, and has added a note on the inaccuracy if the employee has requested it. (Where the employer has not complied with one of those conditions, the court can make such order as it thinks fit to ensure the requirements of para 7 are complied with.)

Right to prevent processing

In certain circumstances, an employee can require a data controller to stop (or not start) processing personal data (DPA 1998, s 10). The grounds are:
* the processing is causing, or is likely to cause, substantial damage or distress to the data subject or someone else; and

- that damage or distress is or would be unwarranted.

The employer must be given written notice of an employee's request, containing reasons, and must be allowed a reasonable period for compliance. Within 21 days of receiving this notice, the employer must give a written response stating that it has complied, or intends to, or stating reasons why the request is unjustified and the extent (if any) to which it has or intends to comply.

There are various exceptions (DPA 1998, Sch 2, paras 1 to 4):

- the employee had given written consent to the processing;
- the processing is necessary for the performance of a contract to which the employee is a party;
- the processing is necessary for taking steps at the employee's request with a view to entering into a contract;
- the processing is necessary for compliance with the employer's non-contractual legal obligations;
- the processing is necessary to protect the employee's vital interests.

If the employer fails to comply with the notice, the employee can seek a court order requiring compliance. The court can make this order if it considers it justified.

The future

However burdensome employers find our current data protection legislation, it looks like there is worse to come. The Employment and Social Affairs Directorate at the EU Commission is proposing a new directive specifically dealing with data protection in the employment context. Early indications are that, despite vocal opposition, the proposals seem to be moving towards law.

The key features of the proposed new directive (based on information circulating, as a formal draft has not yet been published) include the following:

- a body called the 'Article 29 working party' would be given interpretative powers, making it, in effect, a European super-regulator;
- the existing data protection directives would continue to apply to HR data to the extent that issues are not specifically covered by the new directive (for example, the transfer of data overseas);
- the new directive would apply to all manual data used to make decisions about employees – irrespective of whether it was part of a relevant filing system;
- processing of an employee's personal data would be restricted to purposes which were directly relevant and necessary to his employment;
- the use of employee consent for the processing of personal data would be further restricted only to situations where no other legal basis for the processing of data was available;
- the processing of sensitive personal data (including employee health data) would essentially be prohibited (with very limited exceptions);
- routine monitoring of employees would be severely restricted, and the protections afforded by the new directive could not be waived by consent;
- employers would need to ensure that their 'organisational structure' was such that security of personal data was assured;
- consultation with employee representatives would be required prior to the introduction of most employee monitoring;
- any data collected in breach of the directive would be inadmissible in courts and tribunals.

The European legislative process is likely to take at least a couple of years, and the current intention is that the majority of provisions would come into force one year after implementation into UK law, but with certain transitional provisions in relation to manual data held outside a filing system for up to five years.

It will be apparent that should these provisions become law, a significant change in practice and approach to the protection of employee data will be required for employers to remain compliant.

Overview – summary of key concepts

- What is personal data? Does the *Durant* decision change our understanding of the concept?
- What is a relevant filing system? Once again, does *Durant* change our understanding and what are the implications of the proposed EU HR Directive?
- A data subject is any living individual about whom you hold personal data.
- The DPA 1998 covers data controllers who process personal data in the UK, or by reference to a UK establishment.
- Data controllers must comply with the eight data protection principles in relation to the processing of personal data.
- Consent is a problematic issue in data protection terms, obtaining valid consent from existing employees being seen as particularly difficult to achieve.
- Failure to comply with the provisions of the DPA 1998 can lead to enforcement action being taken by the Information Commissioner or court action by aggrieved data subjects.

Chapter 2

Employment records

Susan Henderson

One area in which the Data Protection Act 1998 (the 'DPA 1998') will impact on every employer is in relation to the collection, storage and use of employee records. Employee records might include not only basic information such as name, address and bank details, but also detailed information about an employee's career history, background, health or family.

The purpose of this chapter is to examine the extent to which employers can collect, use and store personal information about their employees.

There is specific provision in Part 4 of the Employment Practices Data Protection Code (the 'Code of Practice') dealing with the collection, use and storage of employees' health information. This is more fully covered in Chapter 3.

Basic legal principles

Underpinning this whole area (as with the rest of data protection law) are the eight data protection principles. These are fully explained in Chapter 1.

In addition, Parts 1 and 2 of the Code of Practice are relevant to the creation and use of employee records. The origin and status of the Code of Practice are explored in the previous chapter.

Audit

The first step in assessing whether an organisation's employment records are held and used in a way which is compliant with the DPA 1998 is to conduct an audit. The organisation needs to know what it has – both on paper and on computer – before it can review that material. At an obvious level, many organisations will have paper and/or electronic personnel files, payroll records or occupational health files. Less obvious sources of personal data might be sickness records, health and safety records, email systems, word processing systems, intranet records or individually held management files.

Useful tools for conducting an audit are available from the Information Commissioner's website (www.informationcommissioner.gov.uk). There is a detailed audit manual which sets out the benefits of conducting an audit and a suggested process for doing so. It also contains useful charts and tables which can be used as a basis for recording the audit results.

Even if an organisation does not want, or does not have the resource, to undertake a full scale audit, at a very basic level every organisation needs to know what systems exist, what information is stored within them and what that information is used for. Once this basic information has been gathered, it is necessary to work out whether the systems are covered by the DPA 1998. (That is, are they relevant filing systems or automated systems?) Do they contain personal data? Is the data sensitive personal data? (This is important as different protections apply to each type of data.) The concepts of 'relevant filing system', 'sensitive personal data' and so on are explained in Chapter 1.

Notification

Once the audit is complete, an organisation will know what records it holds and why it holds them. The next stage is to identify whether notification is required to the Information Commissioner.

The notification requirements are set out in Part III of the DPA 1998. If a data controller should notify and fails to, technically it commits an offence punishable by a fine of up to £5,000 on summary conviction or an unlimited fine on indictment (although to date, so far as the author is aware, no one has actually been prosecuted for this).

Notification is not simply an employment law issue – it applies in relation to any personal data processed by a data controller.

There are certain exemptions from the need to notify, including where the processing is solely for staff administration, keeping the data controller's accounts, or for marketing and public relations (of an organisation's own business – not where products are being marketed to third parties). The number of employers exempt from the need to notify is likely to be very small. However, even where there is no requirement to notify, the data controller must continue to comply with the data protection principles.

A simple online self-assessment form is available from the Information Commissioner's website through which an organisation can check whether or not it needs to notify and then go on to notify online (www.informationcommissioner.gov.uk). At the time of writing notification costs £35 for one year.

There have been stories in the press and indeed warnings issued about unscrupulous organisations which offer to complete the notification process for a data controller and charge a fee of hundreds of pounds for doing so. This is entirely unnecessary. The online notification process is simple, quick and cheap.

General record keeping and purpose statements

The first principle of the DPA 1998 requires:

Personal data shall be processed fairly and lawfully and, in particular, shall not be processed unless –

(a) at least one of the conditions in DPA 1998, Sch 2 is met, and

(b) in the case of sensitive personal data, at least one of the conditions in DPA 1998, Sch 3 is also met.

Part II of DPA 1998, Sch 1 goes on to explain what is meant by fair processing. The main considerations are:

- How was the information obtained? Was it in a fair way? Was it obtained by deception?
- Does the employee know:
  o Who is processing his data?
  o Why the data is being processed?
  o Any further information required in the circumstances to make the processing fair?
- Has the individual been given all of this information in a timely way (that is, when the data is first processed or as soon as practicable thereafter)?

In terms of employment records, this means telling employees

- who you are;
- what information you have about them;
- how it will be used;
- to whom it will be disclosed; and
- where it is to be sent, if outside the EEA.

In addition, where the data being processed is ordinary personal data one of the conditions in DPA 1998, Sch 2 must be satisfied and, if the data is sensitive personal data, one of the conditions in DPA 1998, Sch 3 must be satisfied. DPA 1998, Sch 2 and Sch 3 conditions are explained in Chapter 1.

To satisfy these requirements, organisations are increasingly using 'purpose statements' which are issued to employees (and others whose personal data is processed). These statements will typically set out all of the information required for fair processing and then seek consent for the processing of sensitive personal data or overseas transfer of data where required. An example of a simple purpose statement is set out at Appendix B, although each purpose statement of course needs to be tailored to an organisation's specific needs and may be more or less detailed than the example shown.

A number of practical difficulties arise when dealing with purpose statements:

- How should the statement be communicated to employees (and others)?
  For employees this could be on a notice board, emailed to all employees, on the company intranet, individually issued on paper to each employee, inserted in the staff handbook or contained in some sort of newsletter. The method adopted will be influenced by whether the purpose statement is being used to obtain consent (for example, it is easier to sign and return a piece of paper or reply to an email than it is to signify consent to a document contained in a newsletter). Other considerations might be the need to amend the statement over time (for example, it is easier to amend an electronic document than a paper one). Employers also need to consider what sort of statement should be issued to non-employee workers such as contractors or agency staff whose information is processed but who may not necessarily have access to the same systems as are used to communicate the statement to employees.

- If you are using the purpose statement to obtain consent, what do you do if individuals refuse to sign?
  First, consider what processing really needs consent in the first place. Much use of personal data in the employment context is covered by other conditions for processing in DPA 1998, Sch 2 and Sch 3 and the fact of the processing simply needs to be communicated. If consent really is necessary (for example, for transferring employee information overseas or for processing company sick pay) consider whether it is possible to remove the employee from the system and advise him that you are doing so. If the employee continues to refuse, the options open to an employer are either to remove him from the system or continue the processing anyway in the knowledge that this is a breach of the DPA 1998. Employers may advise employees of the factual consequences of a failure to consent (for example, company sick pay can no longer be paid), but should be careful not to portray this as a threat of a penalty for failure

to consent. For further detail on this issue see Chapter 3 on employees' health.

- How much detail should be included in a purpose statement?

  The answer to this is one of balance. To be entirely compliant with the DPA 1998, an employer should set out in detail each type of information it processes in relation to employees together with the reasons for that processing. If done thoroughly, a statement like this could run to 10 or even 20 pages. This type of statement can be intimidating for employees, can cause suspicion and can take considerable management time in explaining the reasons for introducing the statement. At the other extreme is the very short, one page document which says little more than the identity of the employer, gives some examples of the information held and explains that the information is held and used for employment purposes. This type of statement is easier to explain to employees but is unlikely to achieve full compliance with the first principle of the DPA 1998. For most employers, the answer lies somewhere in the middle – finding a balance between an overly long document which is difficult to sell and a short one which is non-compliant.

What information can an employer collect and keep about employees?

The third principle provides:

> Personal data should be adequate, relevant and not excessive in relation to the purpose or purposes for which [it is] processed.

This principle is fairly self explanatory. In practical terms, don't ask for and collect information you don't need. A classic example is in relation to application forms – the questions 'Are you married?' and 'Do you have children?' are irrelevant to the recruitment decision, are therefore excessive in relation to the purpose of the processing and that data should not be collected. The risk in relation to these particular questions is of course not only in relation to data protection but also sex discrimination law. Similarly, at interviews, the interviewer should not ask

questions or record impressions which are not necessary to the recruitment decision. An employer should not collect or store information just because it might possibly become useful one day.

Recruitment

When advertising for new employees, or collecting application information, organisations need to ensure that they do not fall foul of the data protection principles, notably the first principle (fair and lawful processing) and the third principle (personal data should be adequate, relevant and not excessive). In practice, this means:

- identifying the recruiting company in the advert or application form;
- explaining the purpose for which the information collected in an application form will be used (if it is not obvious);
- obtaining consent to the processing of any sensitive personal data if that is necessary; and
- only asking questions the answers to which are relevant to the recruitment decision.

Once collected, application and recruitment information should only be retained for as long as it is necessary (see further below).

Further detail about the impact of data protection on the recruitment and selection process can be found in the final chapter.

Third party details

Many employment records contain third party details, for example, next of kin information, emergency contact details or family details required for private medical cover. An employer is processing personal information relating to these parties in the same way as it is processing information about employees. Is an employer therefore under an obligation to notify these people in the same way as employees?

> Strictly, in terms of the DPA 1998, an employer is obliged to notify third parties that their information is held (and satisfy one of the conditions for processing in DPA 1988, Sch 2 or 3). In practical terms, however, this presents an employer with

enormous difficulties. One option would of course be to send a copy of the purpose statement to all third parties. In reality this does not happen very often.

The Information Commissioner's office has taken a relatively common sense approach to this problem and for uncontroversial data (such as name, address or contact details) the consent of the employee to the processing of third party information is likely to be acceptable. If, however, the data is sensitive data (such as health information) the explicit consent of the third party is likely to be required (or one of the other DPA 1998, Sch 3 conditions satisfied).

Specific regulations deal with the issue of occupational pension and insurance schemes which hold third party data and provide that the data controller is exempt from the processing obligations in certain contexts. These regulations are outside the scope of this Report.

Keeping personal data accurate and up to date

The fourth data protection principle states:

> Personal data shall be accurate and, where necessary, kept up to date

Personnel files and other employment records can often contain large amounts of out of date information. For example, an employer may hold 30-year-old appointment letters where none of the terms remain relevant to an individual's current role, old salary review notifications or disciplinary warnings which expired many years before. To comply with the fourth principle employers need to follow a two stage process:

(1) Check that the data held is accurate. In the examples given above, all of the information is likely to be accurate. The 30-year-old appointment letter will accurately record the terms of engagement at that time, and the record of the disciplinary warning accurately records its terms.

(2) Even where the information is accurate, is it up to date? In the examples given above none of

the information is up to date. Its useful life has passed and it should no longer be retained.

The principle that records be accurate and up to date is closely related to the fifth data protection principle relating to the retention and destruction of records. The fifth principle is discussed below.

The right to correct inaccurate data

DPA 1998, s 14 gives employees the right to apply to court to have inaccurate data about them corrected, blocked, erased or destroyed. If the application is successful, the employer may have to destroy not only the inaccurate data, but also any opinions based on the inaccurate data and also notify third parties to whom the data has been disclosed.

Data is 'inaccurate' if it is 'incorrect or misleading as to any matter of fact' (DPA 1998, s 70(2)). This means that 'inaccurate' data includes not only information which is factually wrong, but also situations where omissions create a misleading impression.

In deciding whether or not data is inaccurate the court has power to order verification inquiries (DPA 1998, s 14(2)(b)) to test the accuracy of the data.

Retention and destruction of records

The fifth data protection principle states:

> Personal data processed for any purpose or purposes shall not be kept for longer than is necessary for that purpose or those purposes.

This can create tremendous practical difficulties in terms of employment records. How long is it necessary to keep them? The answer requires consideration both of the business and legal position. There will be different retention times for different types of information. Employers need to go back to the audit of records they should have undertaken (see the 'Audit' section above) and consider how long each type of record needs to be retained.

For example:

Type of record	Retention time	Reasoning
Health and safety records in relation to medical examinations of employees exposed to asbestos.	40 years from the examination	Legislation requires records relating to these examinations to be kept for 40 years following the examination.
Basic employment information (dates of service, position, salary)	10 years from termination of employment	Basic employment information is required to give a reference. In certain financial services positions a former employer is under a duty to retain certain information about ex-employees for a specific period of time in order to be able to provide a reference. In companies with final salary pension schemes it may be necessary to retain basic employment information until retirement in case there is a dispute in relation to pension entitlement.
Criminal records bureau certificate	1 month from receipt	A Criminal Records Bureau certificate contains sensitive personal data about an individual's criminal record. It is difficult to see a good reason for retaining anything other than the outcome of the check.
Disciplinary records	12 months from expiry	Disciplinary records normally have a fixed period of time attached to them (for example, a written warning will last for 6 months). It is reasonable to retain the records for a period after they have officially expired to allow the employer to spot any pattern of repeat offending.
Application forms	6 months from recruitment decision	There is a 3-month limit for making most employment claims related to recruitment and it is prudent to add on a little time to allow for the time it takes the employment tribunal to process a claim and for late claims.

It is a question of weighing up the legal, business and regulatory requirements and coming to a view as to how long it is necessary to retain the record. It is important to remember that the fifth data protection principle requires the record to be kept for no longer than is necessary – it is not acceptable to retain records indefinitely simply on the off-chance that they might some day come in useful. Consideration should be given to whether it is the document itself that needs to be retained as opposed to the fact of its existence. For example, after a disciplinary warning has expired it may be sufficient to keep a note on the personnel file of the fact that the warning was given, the type of warning, what it was for and how long it lasted, without needing to keep a copy of the warning letter itself.

No specific limits are set on retention times by the Information Commissioner or the DPA 1998. So, provided an organisation has thought about its requirements and put in place retention times accordingly it should not fall foul of the DPA 1998.

Once the organisation has considered the various types of records it holds and developed retention times for each, a policy should be put in place which sets out the retention times and allocates responsibility for implementing them. When the retention time for a particular set of records has expired they should be securely destroyed.

- From a practical perspective, how can a business manage data retention where the period for which each type of data is to be retained is different?

This is really a matter of common sense. If a judgement is made that one type of data is to be kept for four weeks, another for six weeks, another for three months, another for six months and so on, the process of managing data retention and destruction becomes impossible. When considering the retention policy to be put in places a business therefore needs to consider the practicalities of compliance. This is likely to mean having more uniform retention times which make the data management process easier to handle. Provided the organisation has given some serious thought to the policy, and then actually implements it, the Information Commissioner is unlikely to take enforcement action.

- What happens if we are asked for data which has been destroyed in accordance with our policy on retention and destruction of records?

If the policy is one which has been thought through, and is effectively implemented, then as a data controller you should not be penalised for having deleted or destroyed data in accordance with the data protection principles. The only exception to this is in relation to litigation where you may be under a duty to preserve documents which are relevant to the case and may need to take steps to prevent them being destroyed under the policy.

Email systems can create particular difficulties in relation to the storage and destruction of records. First, the technology used to back up and store email communications is usually relatively crude in that it will take a 'print' of what is on the server at any one time. There is usually no mechanism for filtering the data. The back-up will therefore record everything from emails recording important contractual negotiations to brief personal emails about lunch

appointments or after-work drinks. How can a retention policy be put in place which accurately reflects the useful life of the various types of information retained?

The second problem relates to the difficulty in deleting email. It is very difficult to delete an electronic communication permanently. Even when it looks like the email has disappeared there is often still a record of it somewhere on the computer system.

How then can an employer deal with these issues?

Again, the answer has to be a pragmatic one. The business should consider whether there is any way of filtering information prior to storage or whether there is an alternative way of storing the information which would not require unnecessary data to be kept. If this is not possible and important data (such as contracts) needs to be retrievable by the business for a particular period and these contracts are stored electronically, then it may be that the less important information simply has to be retained for the same period of time as it is not possible to filter it out. There should, however, be some sort of long stop date. The Information Commissioner is unlikely to be impressed with 'forever' as a retention time for any type of data.

At the time of writing, the issue of retention and destruction of data is particularly topical. After the conviction of Ian Huntley for two murders in Soham, it emerged that he had been suspected of nine sexual offences between August 1995 and July 1999. Records of these suspicions had been made although he had never been charged with any offence. Humberside police had deleted these records from their computer on the basis that they thought it was no longer appropriate to keep them taking into account the fifth data protection principle. They said that the DPA 1998 required them to delete information about accusations which did not lead to convictions for the purposes of employment vetting. Had the records been available, it is possible that the police would have questioned Mr Huntley about the murders considerably earlier than they did. The resulting media coverage of the issue focused attention on the ability of the police (and other organisations) to retain and use data and provoked a swift response from the Information Commissioner who took the view that organisations were hiding behind the DPA 1998 to disguise their own shortcomings. His view was that a commonsense approach had to be taken to the retention of information. The DPA 1998 does not impose absolute rules in relation to retention times and it is a question of looking at the information which is held, considering why it is held and then working out its useful life. Clearly it may be useful, and indeed important, to retain records relating to someone who is serially accused of sexual offences for a period of time. This will not offend the fifth data protection principle.

Storage and security of records

The seventh data protection principle states:

> Appropriate technical and organisational measures shall be taken against unauthorised or unlawful processing of personal data and against accidental loss or destruction of, or damage to, personal data.

In the context of employment records this means making sure that employee data (and particularly any sensitive personal data) is only accessible by those who need to see it and is protected from accidental damage. It has even been suggested that employers should comply with ISO 7799 in relation to the storage of employee data. ISO 7799 is a comprehensive and stringent international standard in relation to information security.

In practical terms, some considerations in relation to HR records are:

- For electronic data, what technical security products are on the market – to protect against both unauthorised individuals within the company and also unauthorised third parties gaining access to the data? Are the products effective? Are they expensive? Is their use proportionate within the organisation?
- What products are available in relation to the back up of data? What disaster recovery measures are in place?

- In relation to manual records, are these kept in appropriately locked cabinets? Is access restricted to those who need it? Is there an audit trail showing who has accessed the information and when?
- Are records appropriately separated? For example, not everyone who needs access to an individual's personnel file needs access to their sickness or pension records. Are these stored separately?
- Can the organisation use confidentiality clauses to protect employee data – with those who have access to employee information signing agreements not to disclose the information except where necessary for the performance of their role?
- For employees who use laptops, are adequate measures taken to protect the security of the personal data stored on or accessible from that laptop? Is password protection or some other security software used?

Is an employer obliged to destroy data if an employee asks it to?

An employer is not obliged to destroy personal information about an employee simply because the individual asks it to, provided the information is not inaccurate or irrelevant or held in breach of one or more of the other data protection principles.

An individual does have a very limited right to prevent processing likely to cause him damage or distress – but this right is only available where the damage or distress is unwarranted. DPA 1998, s 10 sets out the procedure for exercising the right.

For example, if a former employee doesn't want basic employment details held about him (for no good reason) and the employer holds those details for the purpose of being able to give references or for tax purposes, then the employee has no right to require them to be destroyed. However, if an employee doesn't want her new home phone number put on to the employee intranet because of fears of domestic violence from a former partner then she will probably be able to prevent the processing.

Outsourcing and other third party providers

Organisations are increasingly using third party providers to outsource functions such as human resources or payroll. Third party providers are also used in relation to pension provision, health insurance, employee assistance programmes and a number of other employee benefits. In order for these functions or benefits to operate effectively, the employer must pass on to the third party employee data which, in the case of health or pension provision, will often be sensitive personal data.

In determining what obligations an employer has in relation to these records, the first step is to determine whether the third party is a 'data controller' or a 'data processor'. The distinction between these two terms is fully explored in Chapter 1.

If the third party is a data controller (as is likely to be the case with a pension or healthcare provider) then the third party is responsible for ensuring that its use of the employee information is in accordance with the DPA 1998. The obligation of the employer would simply extend to telling employees that their information was being passed on or, where appropriate, getting employee consent to the data being passed on.

If, on the other hand, the third party is a data processor (as is likely to be the case with a payroll or HR provider) then the employer retains responsibility for ensuring that the processing of the employee data by the third party is in accordance with the DPA 1998. A contract needs to be put in place which specifies the uses the data processor can make of the information and imposes adequate security safeguards. The employer, as data controller, must then check that the third party is complying with those obligations.

When data is passed to third parties the employer should ensure that it is the minimum amount of information necessary for the purpose.

Treatment of criminal record information

There is a very restricted ability for some employers to obtain information about the criminal record of current or prospective employees.

The ability to obtain this information is highly regulated – only employers who are employing individuals in exempted positions under the Rehabilitation of Offenders Act 1974 (that is, people who work with children or vulnerable adults, or employees in exempt professions like lawyers or vets in respect of whom you can ask about spent convictions) can make the request. These employers are entitled to become 'registered bodies' with the Criminal Records Bureau.

The request needs to be directed to the Criminal Records Bureau which currently issues 'standard' and 'enhanced' disclosure certificates showing the criminal record and certain other information relating to individuals who are to be employed in an exempt position.

The Criminal Records Bureau will only respond to requests from registered bodies (or requests made through an appropriate umbrella organisation) and the certificate will be sent direct to the registered body with a copy to the individual.

A third category of disclosure certificate called a 'basic' disclosure which would list all unspent criminal convictions and would be suitable for more general employment use is due to be introduced. The idea when the Criminal Records Bureau was set up was that only an individual would be able to apply for a basic disclosure about himself (not an employer and not a registered body). It would then to be up to the individual whether or not he showed that disclosure to anyone.

Following a recent consultation on the issue, the introduction of basic disclosures looks far from imminent. The Criminal Records Bureau is overstretched and is struggling to cope with its current obligations in relation to standard and enhanced disclosures. There have been indications that the introduction of the basic disclosure will be delayed until the Criminal Records Bureau can cope with its current workload. There have also been suggestions that the basic disclosure will no longer be available direct to individuals, but that applications will have to be made through registered bodies so that the identity of the individual can be verified.

Further detailed information in relation to disclosure certificates and the Criminal Records Bureau is available from the Criminal Records Bureau website (www.disclosure.gov.uk), and on the exempt positions under the Rehabilitation of Offenders Act 1974 from the Home Office website (www.homeoffice.gov.uk).

At present, if an employer is not employing individuals in an exempt position the only way of obtaining criminal record information about employees is to ask the employee to produce that information himself. Employers should think carefully before asking for criminal record information, however, to avoid breaching the data protection principles. First, is the collection of the information really necessary? If it is not necessary to the position then the employer should not be collecting the information in any event. If the information is necessary, the DPA 1998 would suggest that you just ask the question on an application form and take no further steps to verify the data obtained unless there is a particular reason to distrust the answer given. The process of making an individual obtain a copy of his criminal record from the police for the purpose of showing it to his employer is an example of 'enforced subject access'.

When the provisions relating to basic disclosure come into force (which could be years from now) enforced subject access will become an offence under the DPA 1998.

If criminal record information is obtained (whether through disclosure or by asking the employee), it should not be kept for longer than is necessary for the purpose for which it was obtained.

In Scotland, the equivalent service to the Criminal Records Bureau is Disclosure Scotland which operates in a very similar way. Further details can be found on its website (www.disclosure scotland.org.uk).

Third party information requests

It can be a criminal offence for an individual to disclose personal data about a fellow employee to a third party. Information should only be disclosed if (1) there is a legal obligation to do so or (2) it is fair to do so. There are examples of situations where individuals use deception to try to obtain information, so it is very important to verify the identity of anyone seeking employee information, preferably in writing, before providing it to others.

Often, requests are made by the police or a government department in relation to employees. Do not simply assume that because an official body is asking for the information that it is fair to disclose it. Check the request in the same way as you would for any other organisation or person.

The issue of passing information to third parties has been in the news recently. One case involved two pensioners who lived in Tooting, South London. They were found dead in their home on 18 October 2003, having been dead for several weeks. Their gas supply had been cut off in August 2003. British Gas claimed that it could not inform social services that the supply was cut off because the DPA 1998 required it to obtain a customer's consent before information relating to a debt was passed on to a third party.

The response of the Information Commissioner to this incident was to try to encourage a common sense approach. He has warned companies not to hide behind the DPA 1998 to disguise their own shortcomings.

International data management

Multinational companies will commonly need and want to transfer employment records between locations in different countries. The restrictions on an organisation's ability to do this together with the potential solutions are explored in Chapter 7.

Employment records – summary of main issues

- Consider whether notification under DPA 1998 Part III is required in relation to the types of processing undertaken by the business.
- Consider the use of purpose statements as a method of complying with the obligation to process personal data fairly and lawfully.
- Ensure that no more information is kept about employees than is necessary for the effective running of the business.
- Put in place a policy and procedure relating to the retention and destruction of employment records which makes sense in the context of the business.
- Check whether adequate security measures are in place in relation to the protection of employment records.

Chapter 3

Information about employees' health

Rachel Mann

Employers will need to process information about employees' health for several legitimate reasons. However, employers must take extra care when processing this type of information. There are two reasons for this. First, such information is not merely 'personal data' but it is 'sensitive personal data'. (A full discussion of the meaning of sensitive personal data can be found in Chapter 1.) Secondly, from a practical perspective, employees are likely to be very concerned about the sharing of information about their health. Many individuals consider such details to be extremely private and employers should remember that one of the primary purposes of the Data Protection Act 1998 ('the DPA 1998') is to protect privacy in personal data. The Information Commissioner comments that it will be intrusive and may be highly intrusive to obtain information about employees' health. Employers should be mindful of these comments.

Guiding principles

All of the data protection principles contained in DPA 1998, Sch 1 (fully explained in Chapter 1) apply to the processing of information about employees' health. However, the first three principles tend to be the most relevant.

In addition, the Information Commissioner has dedicated one part of the Employment Practices Data Protection Code, (the 'Code of Practice'), Part 4, to information about employees' health. Employers should note that Part 4 is still in draft form and is not due to be finalised until July 2004, so the comments in this Report are based on the current version which may be revisited in some respects. At present, there is some tension between the various parts of the Code of Practice. Part 2, which deals with employment records, was written by the previous Information Commissioner, Elizabeth France. Although Part 4 is specifically dedicated to information about employees' health, Part 2 covers sickness and accident records and takes a different approach from Part 4. The differences will be discussed below in the section on 'Sickness and absence records', but where there is conflict it seems sensible for employers to rely predominantly on Part 4, being the most recently issued part of the Code of Practice and the part that specifically deals with information about employees' health. The Information Commissioner has also published Supplementary Guidance to complement Part 4 of the Code of Practice. The Supplementary Guidance is available from the Information Commissioner's website (www.informationcommissioner.gov.uk under Codes of Practice) or by telephoning 01625 545745.

Medical records are a sub-set of records generally held by employers. Therefore, the principles discussed in the employment records chapter relating to the retention and use of employment records are also applicable to medical records. This chapter only deals with the specific additional issues arising in connection with medical records.

Information about employees' health

The most obvious example of information which employers will hold about their employees' health is their sickness records. However, the following are also examples of information which an employer may hold about its employees' health:

- pre-employment medical questionnaires;
- information received from an employee, or a health professional, about an employee's disability with suggestions for reasonable adjustments to be made for that employee;
- the results of an eye test taken by an employee using VDU equipment;
- records of an employee's blood type kept by an industrial employer in case the employee is involved in an accident;
- records of blood tests carried out to ensure that an employee has not been exposed to hazardous substances;
- drug or alcohol test results;
- genetic test results.

Obtaining information about employees' health

The first data protection principle (DPA 1998, Sch 1) provides:

> Personal data shall be processed fairly and lawfully and, in particular, shall not be processed unless:
> (a) at least one of the conditions in Schedule 2 is met; and
> (b) in the case of sensitive personal data, at least one of the conditions in Schedule 3 is also met.

Therefore, for an employer lawfully to hold information about its employees' health, one of the conditions from each of DPA 1998, Sch 2 and Sch 3 must be satisfied. As Sch 3 conditions are more restrictive, if one of them is satisfied it is very common that a Sch 2 condition is also satisfied. This chapter therefore concentrates on Sch 3 conditions.

The most relevant conditions in DPA 1998, Sch 3 are:

1. the employee has given his explicit consent;
2. processing is necessary for the employer to comply with a legal obligation which is connected with the employment;
3. the processing is necessary to protect the vital interests of the employee in certain circumstances, for example where the employee is involved in an accident, is unconscious and in a critical condition;
4. the processing is necessary for the purpose of taking legal advice, or in connection with actual or prospective legal proceedings (most likely when defending tribunal claims); and
5. the processing is necessary for medical purposes and is undertaken by a health professional or someone who owes an equivalent duty of confidentiality.

Consent

Obtaining consent or explicit consent is difficult. To be able to give 'explicit' consent, the employee must have been clearly told the nature of the information about his health which will be held and the purpose for which it will be used. (This is in any event necessary to comply with the first data protection principle so should be done even if consent is not sought.) The employee must then give a positive indication of his agreement to the processing of that information, for example by signing a consent form. The difficulties associated with obtaining consent are fully explored in Chapter 1.

So what is an employer to do in practice? There appear to be three options:
1. Explain the issue to the employees and seek their consent;
2. Inform the employees but do not seek their consent;
3. Rely on another Sch 3 condition.

There are difficulties with each of these options.

1. **Explain the issue to the employees and seek their consent**

   As explained in Chapter 1, there are issues as to whether consent is likely to be freely given and it could therefore be invalid.

   There is also the problem of how to deal with employees who refuse consent. An employer can try to remove the employees' health data from the employer's databases but this is fraught with practical and legal problems from other perspectives. The employer will find some health records useful in ensuring it complies with its duties not to dismiss unfairly or discriminate on the grounds of disability.

   If an employer asks for consent but then tells the employee it is going to process his health data anyway, it is likely to damage the employer/ employee relationship. In extreme circumstances an employee may be sufficiently upset by this to consider it a fundamental breach of his contract of employment and use it as the basis of a constructive dismissal claim. Alternatively, or in addition, the employee could report the employer to the Information Commissioner.

   If an employer does seek to rely on consent it should ensure the consent covers not only any testing or other collection of medical information but also its recording, use and disclosure.

2. **Inform employees but do not seek their consent**

   Giving the employees information as to the type of health information which will be held about them, how it will be held and used and to whom it will be disclosed forms part of an employer's obligations in any event. Some employers may question the point of attempting to seek consent which is unlikely to be valid for data protection purposes. Not seeking consent means the employer may not have to deal with difficult consequences arising out of refusals to consent. Of course, employees may object anyway once they are informed. Practically, such objections are unlikely if employees feel that their employer is using their health information appropriately, although disgruntled employees may relish a reason to make trouble.

   This approach suffers from the certain defect that it does not comply with the DPA 1998.

3. **Rely on another Sch 3 condition**

The only other Sch 3 condition which is likely to be useful is compliance with an obligation imposed by law. This condition is discussed further below. It may not be broad enough to cover all the purposes for which an employer will want to process health information.

If employers choose to rely on another Sch 3 condition, they should still ensure that their employees are fully aware of what information is being sought about their health, how it is being held and who has access to that information. In addition to duties under the DPA 1988, this is relevant for complying with the employer's duty of trust and confidence.

Whichever approach is adopted, employers should comply with all the other data protection principles. The current Information Commissioner has repeatedly stated that he wants to take a common sense approach to the DPA 1998 and its enforcement. If an employer is complying in all other respects and can justify why it has decided to adopt one of the above approaches, it is hoped the Information Commissioner will be sympathetic and approach breaches leniently. The unfortunate truth is that as the law and the Code of Practice currently stand, there is great difficulty in reconciling an employer's obligations under the DPA 1998 and other legislation in the context of processing health information.

When an employer wants a report from a doctor who cares for an employee, for instance a GP or a specialist, it may also need to get consent under the Access to Medical Reports Act 1988 ('AMRA 1988'). Under AMRA 1988, the employee has the right to:

- see the report before it is sent to the employer/ employer's Occupational Health Department;
- request that the report be amended; and
- refuse consent for it to be disclosed to the employer/employer's Occupational Health Department.

Compliance with an obligation imposed by law

As indicated, this is one of the conditions contained in DPA 1998, Sch 3 which allows processing of sensitive personal data.

DPA 1998, Sch 2 conditions differentiate between contractual and non-contractual legal obligations, whereas the second condition in DPA 1998, Sch 3 merely refers to an obligation imposed by law on the employer. Therefore, it is arguable that this Sch 3 condition could be read to include a contractual legal obligation as it fails to exclude it expressly as the third Sch 2 condition does.

However, in his Supplementary Guidance, the Information Commissioner only interprets this condition in the context of employers' obligations imposed by statute or common law. Examples of these are the obligations:

- to provide a safe working environment;
- not to discriminate on the grounds of disability; and
- not to dismiss employees when it would be unfair to do so.

It is very important for employers to remember that most of the conditions in DPA 1998, Sch 3 require that the particular processing is **necessary** for the relevant purpose. What is 'necessary' is not always obvious. An easy example: if the purpose of providing a safe working environment can be achieved by completion of a questionnaire rather than by requiring employees to take a drug test, the condition will not be satisfied and the processing of the test results will be unlawful under the DPA 1998.

When does the processing of health information become necessary for the purpose of not unfairly dismissing an employee? Arguably, not until the employer is considering dismissing the employee. However, if the dismissal is for persistent short-term absences, the employer should have followed a warning process and so will have needed details of absences to conduct the process. It may not necessarily have needed details of the **reason** for the absences in this circumstance. On the other hand, if the dismissal is for capability due to long-term absence, then the reason for the absence and the prognosis, will be highly relevant. Such information will have probably been needed for some time for the employer to comply with other duties: to support the employee, provide reasonable adjustments and generally manage him appropriately.

One practical difficulty is that an employer may only know with hindsight which data is relevant to the dismissal decision. Again, this is something of a no-win situation. Employers are urged to comply with the spirit of the DPA 1998 and adopt a common sense approach following proper consideration of their obligations.

Impact assessments

Satisfying one of the conditions under DPA 1998, Sch 3 is not the end of the process. The Information Commissioner advises in the Code of Practice that employers should also conduct an 'impact assessment'. The purpose of an impact assessment is to assess whether the benefits of processing the information about employees' health justify the intrusion into their privacy or any other adverse impact on them. Impact assessments are also used in other areas, particularly monitoring (see the chapter on monitoring). An impact assessment requires an employer to:

- identify clearly the **purpose(s)** for which the health information is to be collected and held and the benefits that this is likely to deliver;
- identify any likely **adverse impact**;
- consider **alternatives**;
- take into account the **obligations** that arise; and
- finally, judge whether collecting and holding the health information is **justified** in the circumstances.

We look at each of these in turn.

Clear purposes

Most employers will be fully aware of the purpose for which they want the information about their employees' health. However, employers should consider who collects the information and restrict this as appropriate to ensure that only information necessary to meet the purpose is collected, and that it is only disclosed to those who need to know (see discussion of the third data protection principle (DPA 1998, Sch 1) in the section on 'Relevant information' below).

Adverse impact

The potential adverse impact is not limited to the employee, but extends to anyone who may be affected by it, most obviously the employee's family. For example, a pre-employment medical examination or a genetic test may reveal the existence of or a pre-disposition to a terminal illness which will clearly affect the employee's family as well as the employee himself.

Alternatives

The aspect of an impact assessment which is often overlooked is that of considering alternatives. This links back to the discussion about whether the planned method of collecting the information is 'necessary'. It may be that there is a less intrusive way of achieving the same purpose, for example completion of a health questionnaire rather than provision of a blood sample.

Consideration of legal obligations

The obligations that arise from obtaining and processing information about employees' health primarily focus on whether, and if so how, the information will be communicated to the relevant employee and on ensuring that the information is securely stored. For example, if tests have revealed an unknown illness, this information must be considerately notified to the employee. The employer may need to consider whether it is appropriate to provide counselling. With regard to the security of the information, the general principles explained in the chapter on employment records apply. In particular, thought should be given to the question of who will have access to the health information. This should be severely restricted. The Information Commissioner suggests in the Code of Practice that health information should be restricted to medical professionals wherever possible and that line managers will normally only need to know an individual's prognosis, namely information relating to when they are likely to be able to return to work.

Bearing in mind employers' other obligations, this approach may be unduly restrictive. There will be circumstances, particularly where somebody has a disability, where the line manager will need to know the details of the illness to be able to manage the employee compassionately and appropriately and to contribute productively to discussions about reasonable adjustments that can be made to assist the employee.

The general principle is that people should only have access to information about employees' health on a 'need-to-know basis'. For the same reason, line managers should be discouraged from sending emails to occupational health doctors requesting information about employees' health as IT employees may have access to such emails, especially if the email system is monitored. Therefore, a more appropriate means of communication to and from occupational health doctors may be by private and confidential letter.

The Information Commissioner also suggests in the Code of Practice that information about employees' health should be kept separately from other personnel information (for example by keeping it in a sealed envelope) or be subject to additional access controls where it is held electronically. It may be more practical to keep manual records in a locked file cabinet.

Justification

The final stage of the impact assessment is to consider whether collection of that particular type of information about an employee's health is justified given the intrusion to his privacy.

The Information Commissioner acknowledges that undertaking an impact assessment need not be a complicated or an onerous process. In simple cases, he says that it merely requires a mental evaluation of the risks of the individual situation and whether the benefit of obtaining the information would sufficiently reduce those risks to justify the invasion into the employee's privacy. Documentation evidencing the process followed may be needed in

more complicated circumstances. From a practical perspective it obviously helps if an employer keeps some form of written record to evidence that an impact assessment has actually been conducted. However, the fundamental point is that consideration should be given to whether that particular form of intrusion is necessary and appropriate in the individual circumstances.

Use of information about employees' health

The second data protection principle (DPA 1998, Sch 1) states:

> Personal data shall be obtained only for one or more specified and lawful purposes, and shall not be further processed in any manner incompatible with that purpose or those purposes.

Given this principle, employers should ensure that when they notify employees of the purpose for which information about their health is being collected, all of the relevant purposes are identified. A classic situation where this principle can be breached is where information about an employee's health has been collected for the purposes of a pension scheme or an insurance benefit, but is then made available to the employer who relies on it for another reason, for example reviewing the employee's absences from the office.

To ensure that such cross-communication does not occur, it may be helpful to ask employees to provide information about their health either direct to the pension provider or the insurer or, if it must go via the employer, in a sealed envelope not to be opened by the employer.

Relevant information

The third data protection principle (DPA 1998, Sch 1) indicates that:

> Personal data shall be adequate, relevant and not excessive in relation to the purpose or purposes for which [it is] processed.

This principle could easily be breached by the use of a pre-employment medical questionnaire which has not been tailored to the particular employment. For example, it is easy to understand why an employer would need to know about a history of heart disease or epilepsy from an employee applying to be a forklift truck driver. However, the same could not necessarily be said if the employee was applying for a sedentary office job. Employers who use health questionnaires should therefore ensure that they are regularly checked and are appropriate to the particular employment. It is suggested that this is most appropriately conducted by a health professional rather than, for example, a member of the personnel department. The health professional can then simply confirm whether the individual is or is not suitable for the proposed employment.

In some situations, particularly in the context of tribunal litigation, an employer may request disclosure of a GP's notes about an employee. Of course, a GP is under a common law duty of confidence (*Hunter v Mann* [1974] QB 767), together with any professional confidentiality obligations. This means that he may not voluntarily disclose information which he has gained in his professional capacity without the patient's consent. Therefore, if an employer wants disclosure of a GP's records for the purposes of tribunal litigation, it will need either the employee's consent or a tribunal order for disclosure. Tribunals may order the production of documents under the Employment Tribunals Rules of Procedure, r 4(5)(a), the Employment Tribunals (Constitution and Rules of Procedure) Regulations 2001 (SI 2001/1171), Sch 1.

Some of a GP's notes may be relevant and it may be entirely proper that they are disclosed. However, it is highly likely that the GP's notes will also contain information about other aspects of the employee's health that bear no relation to the issue in which the employer has a legitimate interest. Therefore, employers should ensure that when they ask employees to consent to, or tribunals to order, the disclosure of medical notes they are specific as to

the condition about which they are seeking information.

Sickness and accident records

As mentioned in the 'Guiding principles' section, sickness and accident records are currently covered under Part 2 of the Code of Practice. Part 2 of the Code of Practice follows the old format of 'benchmarks' which are effectively a fairly prescriptive list of do's and don't's. The Information Commissioner has indicated that he will be reviewing the old parts of the Code of Practice (including Part 2). Therefore Part 2 may change and perhaps become more in line with Part 4, the format of which is more focused on guidance with suggested actions.

One benchmark in Part 2 of the Code of Practice states that sickness and accident records should be kept separately from absence records, and that sickness records should not be used where simple records of absence would suffice. For example, payroll staff need only know the number of days of absence, not the reason, to be able to calculate the appropriate statutory sick pay entitlement.

Another important benchmark states that sickness, accident or absence records of individual employees should not be made available to other employees, except in the case of managers who may receive information about members of their team to the extent that this is necessary to carry out their managerial roles.

Once again, it is easy to see a tension between best practice from a data protection perspective and ensuring that disabled employees are not discriminated against. Of course, an employer does not have to know that an employee is suffering from a disability for duties under the Disability Discrimination Act 1995 to arise; it is sufficient that it knows the symptoms from which the employee is suffering. Often the line manager will be in the best position to evaluate behaviour, but may not recognise the issue as a potential disability if he is unaware of the reason for the employee's absence. It is arguable that a manager will be unable to fulfil his duties without such information and therefore is entitled to receive it without breaching the Code of Practice.

Other guidance from the Information Commissioner is less controversial, for example 'league tables' of sickness absences should not be published. Most people would agree that the intrusion of privacy would be disproportionate to any managerial benefit gained from such presentation of information about employees' health. If an employer genuinely thinks that it has a problem with high levels of absence, it is quite permissible to collate sickness absences by department or section, providing this is done in such a way that individual employees cannot be identified from this information.

Occupational health schemes

Many employers have occupational health departments or relationships with local surgeries under which they nominate doctors as company doctors. (For the purposes of this chapter all such arrangements are referred to as 'occupational health departments'.) All medical personnel working in occupational health departments will clearly be covered by their own duties of confidentiality to the patients. In addition, they will need to comply with the *Guidance on the Ethics for Occupational Physicians* (5th edn, May 1999, Faculty of Occupational Medicine, ISBN 1-86016-112-X).

Occupational health departments are useful to employers for several reasons. Occupational health staff generally know the working conditions well and so can advise in a more informed manner as to whether an employee is fit to return to the working environment or what adjustments are most practicable. In addition, appropriate use of occupational health departments helps employers comply with one of the Information Commissioner's core principles in the Code of Practice. He advises that the assessment of the implications of an employee's health or fitness for work should normally be left to a suitably qualified health professional.

It is particularly important that it is made clear to employees if any information which they provide to

the health professionals in occupational health departments will be communicated to line managers or to members of the employer's personnel department. Unless they are told otherwise, employees have the right to assume that any information that they give to such health professionals will be given in confidence and will not be passed on. This is not only from the data protection perspective but also because of the occupational health personnel's duty of confidence to patients. However, from the employer's perspective, the purpose of referring an employee to the occupational health department is usually to obtain guidance as to the employee's diagnosis and prognosis and the support which the employer can provide. Therefore, employees should be asked to consent to occupational health professionals providing line managers with reports restricted to those types of issues. Assurances should be given that other information disclosed by employees to occupational health professionals will not be disclosed (unless the employees agree).

Employers need to ensure that they do receive all necessary information from their occupational health departments. In the context of disability discrimination, knowledge of an employer's occupational health department will be deemed to be within the employer's knowledge (*H J Heinz Co Ltd v Kenrick* [2000] IRLR 144 at 149). Therefore, employers are well advised to ensure their employees consent to occupational health professionals providing reports to line managers along the lines described above.

Occupational health records may need to be kept for a considerable length of time pursuant to health and safety legislation. For example, documents which relate to the control of substances hazardous to health, lead and asbestos at work have to be kept for 40 years from the date of the last entry and those relating to ionising radiations have to be kept for 50 years[1]. The records have to be kept securely throughout this time. As conditions which arise from such workplace risks often do not emerge for many years, the Health and Safety Executive recommends that employers should give employees copies of their individual occupational health records when they leave employment. (See for example the HSE Information Sheet 'Radiation doses – assessment and recording' available on the Health & Safety Executive's website – www.hse.gov.uk.)

Medical examination and testing

The Information Commissioner states in the section of the Code of Practice dealing with medical examination and testing that employees should know:

- the circumstances in which medical testing may take place;
- the nature of the testing;
- how the information obtained through the testing will be used; and
- what safeguards are in place.

As expected, the Information Commissioner reminds us that medical examination or testing should only be used where the testing is necessary and justified. He suggests that medical examination or testing of current employees should only occur as part of a voluntary occupational health and safety programme, unless the employer is satisfied that such examination or testing is necessary and justified:

- to prevent a significant risk to the health and safety of the employee, or others;
- to determine the employee's fitness for continued employment;
- to determine the employee's entitlement to health related benefits such as sick pay;
- to prevent discrimination against the employee on grounds of disability; or
- for the purposes of establishing whether the employee is eligible to join a pension or insurance scheme.

The Information Commissioner suggests that employers should record the business purpose for which the particular examination or test is being introduced.

It would be advisable for employers to include in their staff handbook or other communication sent to all employees the purpose of medical examinations that they may be asked to undergo,

the types of examination or test, the uses to which the information obtained from such an examination or test will be put and to whom the information will be disclosed. If the employer has done so, this will form good evidence to the Information Commissioner that the employer has thought through the reasons for needing medical testing and also conveyed them to the workforce. However, employers should take care that if any further examinations or testing are needed for a different purpose, the employees are informed of all of the above aspects of those additional examinations or tests.

An employer should have conducted an impact assessment, as discussed in the 'Impact assessment' section, to establish that there are no less intrusive methods of obtaining the necessary information than by medical examination or testing.

The second data protection principle (DPA 1998, Sch 1) (which requires that data is only processed for the purpose for which it was collected) is highly relevant to medical examination and testing. If a urine sample is taken, for example, for the purpose of testing whether someone is diabetic, the sample must not also be tested to see if the employee is pregnant. Wherever possible tests should be used which only divulge information relevant to the purpose for which the test was carried out. If other information will be disclosed by the testing this should be ignored. The employer may discover that it has a legitimate reason for needing to undertake a second test on an existing sample from the employee. In this case, the employer should inform the employee and obtain his consent to the second test before conducting it.

In addition to breaching the DPA 1998, if an employer tested a medical sample without the employee's consent for that particular testing, it would also be acting in breach of Sch 1, Art 8 of the Human Rights Act 1998 (the 'HRA 1998') (X v EC Commission [1995] IRLR 320). Breach of the HRA 1998 on its own is only actionable if the breach is by a public authority. However, if the breach were by a private employer, the employee might attempt to use the breach to argue, for example, that his dismissal for a positive test was unfair. Private employers may also want to ensure that they do not breach the HRA 1998, as if they do, even if they do not breach any of the other data protection principles, the first data protection principle will be breached because the information will not have been collected lawfully. Therefore, breach of the HRA 1998 may be problematic for private employers even when they are dealing with employees with less than one year's service or job applicants.

Drug and alcohol testing

The points in the previous section regarding medical testing obviously also apply to drug and alcohol testing. The Information Commissioner also gives specific guidance about drug and alcohol testing. He considers that such testing is unlikely to be justified unless it is for health and safety reasons.

When considering whether drug or alcohol testing is justified on health and safety grounds employers should consider the following issues both from a data protection perspective and from a human rights viewpoint. Employers normally want to test for drugs because they consider that their use will endanger the safety of the employee himself or his colleagues or customers. However, not only illegal substances affect an employee's ability to perform certain activities safely, such as driving. Many prescription only medicines (also called 'POMs') and several pharmacy (also called 'P') medicines warn against the dangers of drowsiness and state that if the patient is affected in this way he should not drive or operate machinery. Therefore, if an employer wants to conduct tests to establish if someone's ability to drive is impaired, it should not merely focus on illegal substances.

The employer must also consider carefully whether the information provided by the test will actually establish the risk. For example, a test which merely establishes the presence of a substance rather than its level will be of limited use in establishing whether that individual is a risk to safety.

In the Information Commissioner's Supplementary Guidance, he indicates that other than in the most safety critical areas, regular drug testing is unlikely to be justified unless there is a reasonable suspicion

that drug use has an impact on safety. As with all areas, employers must consider whether there is a less intrusive method of establishing whether an employee's ability is impaired. For example, equipment exists which can measure hand-eye co-ordination and response time. These alternatives may in fact address a safety risk better than drug testing as they may identify poor hand-eye co-ordination from any cause.

Unsurprisingly, the Information Commissioner points out that even within the same type of industry or business not all employees will pose the same risk to safety if they are impaired by the use of drug or alcohol. For example, a drunk train driver is clearly a far greater risk to safety than a drunk ticket collector.

As drug and alcohol testing is so intrusive, the Information Commissioner suggests that employers would be well advised to document an impact assessment (see the 'Impact assessment' section). (This would also be helpful evidence if an employee alleged a breach of the HRA 1998.)

Covert drug and alcohol testing is difficult from a practical perspective, but has apparently been tried by some employers. (In this context covert testing includes both obtaining a sample covertly and covertly testing a sample given for another reason). In line with the Information Commissioner's view on covert monitoring (see Chapter 5 on monitoring), he indicates that covert testing may only be carried out in exceptional circumstances which would invariably include police involvement.

Clearly, if employers are going to test for drug and alcohol use they will need to ensure that the tests they use are reliable. With the exception of using a breathalyser to detect the presence of alcohol, such tests should be conducted by a qualified health professional. To ensure that the fourth data protection principle (DPA 1998, Sch 1) (relating to accuracy of data) is complied with, a secure chain of custody for samples must be ensured.

The Information Commissioner does accept that there are some very limited circumstances in which employers may be justified in testing to detect the **presence** of an illegal substance rather than testing to establish impairment on health and safety grounds. He gives two examples. First, where illegal drug use is a breach of the employee's contract of employment or disciplinary rules. Secondly, where illegal use could cause substantial damage to the employer's business.

This second example is the argument most commonly used by many employers as to why they want to introduce drug and alcohol testing. However, the example that the Information Commissioner gives in this context is 'seriously undermining public confidence in the integrity of a law enforcement agency'. This suggests that the Information Commissioner will not necessarily be persuaded that the preservation of the reputation of a private company is sufficient justification for testing for illegal substances.

In addition to information about the purposes of drug and alcohol testing, employees must also know the consequences of a positive test. It is a matter of good employment practice in any event to have a drug and/or alcohol policy in a Staff Handbook or other communication issued to all employees. This is particularly the case if the employer wishes to test for the presence of these substances. The policy should obviously explain the consequences of breaching the rules. Such policies need to be specific, for example will an employee be disciplined for having alcohol in his blood regardless of the amount or only if he is over the legal limit for driving? Are there some circumstances in which the consumption of alcohol is acceptable, such as employer sponsored social events? Is there a system of warning or is a first offence considered gross misconduct justifying dismissal? The sanction may of course depend on the extent or level of misuse.

Genetic testing

Genetic tests are considerably less common than other forms of medical testing, but they are becoming somewhat more popular with employers, especially those with US parent companies. Generally, employers want to test job applicants to establish whether they have a pre-disposition to developing particular illnesses. An employer might want to know

because some illnesses may jeopardise the health and safety of other employees or simply because such an employee is likely to cost the employer more in sickness benefits.

Genetic testing is still in a developmental stage. The predictive value of genetic testing is quite limited. There are some diseases which result from a defect in a single gene, such as cystic fibrosis, sickle cell anaemia, Huntingdon's disease and haemophilia. However, such diseases do not affect a large percentage of the population. Other diseases such as heart disease, several cancers and some allergies, which are thought to result from the interactions between several genes, are also complicated by other influences such environment, diet and lifestyle. Therefore testing for such diseases is virtually impossible at present. Even testing for those diseases which result from a defect in a single gene cannot predict whether the disease will actually manifest itself during the working life of the employee, nor can such testing predict the severity of the future disease.

In light of the above, it is unsurprising that the Information Commissioner states that genetic testing should not be used to make predictions about an employee's future general health. His reasoning for this is both that it is too intrusive and that its predictive value is insufficiently certain to be relied on to provide accurate information. The Information Commissioner does accept that genetic tests may be appropriate to a particular employee with a particular detectable genetic condition which is likely to pose a serious threat to safety, or where employees are in a specific working environment which might pose specific risks to employees with a particular genetic condition. An example of this is the Ministry of Defence which tests for sickle cell disease because someone who suffers from that condition may have a crisis provoked by low oxygen pressure in flights. (Another consideration which employers must bear in mind if they are considering genetic testing is the potential for indirect sex or race discrimination. For example, sickle cell disease is more prevalent in those of Afro-Caribbean origin.)

In the context of genetic testing, considering alternatives as part of an impact assessment will be critical. Genetic testing should clearly only be used as a last resort where there are no other alternatives. If the safety risk is to the employee only, then an employer should not force that employee to undergo a genetic test. As part of the employer's duty of trust and confidence it should of course provide all the information to the particular employee as to why it thinks that there might be a risk. The employee may then make an informed choice as to whether or not he wishes to submit to a genetic test.

As with all medical testing, the accuracy and the reliability of the test and the skill and experience of the person conducting the test must be paramount.

When undertaking the impact assessment for possible genetic testing, an employer must pay careful attention to the obligations which would arise. If the genetic test is positive, the employer is likely to find its health and safety obligations increased in respect of that particular employee given the information that it now has about his condition. This additional information will have to be considered when undertaking risk assessments and exposing the employee to occupational hazards. An employer would also be very well advised to provide appropriate counselling and support mechanisms to prevent a successful claim for negligence or personal injury on the basis of psychiatric damage caused by positive test results being notified to the employee.

Finally, the Information Commissioner states that employees should not be required to disclose the results of previous genetic tests, so that they are not put off having tests which may be beneficial to their health by the fear that they will have to disclose the results to a current or future employer.

The future

The general approach to data protection may become less restrictive as a result of case law such as the Court of Appeal's decision in *Durant v Financial Services Authority* [2003] EWCA Civ 1746, [2003] All ER (D) 124 (Dec) (see Chapter 1 for a full discussion) and the current Information Commissioner's common sense approach. However, this relaxation is unlikely to apply to information about employees' health. As mentioned at the beginning of this chapter, such information is intensely private and its processing is likely to remain highly regulated.

Information about employees' health – summary of main issues

- Information about employees' health is sensitive personal data and intensely private.
- One of the Sch 3 conditions should be satisfied before an employer processes information about employees' health. However, this is very difficult to achieve and in practice employers may have to settle for an 'as compliant as possible' approach.
- Employers should conduct an impact assessment to establish if holding particular types of information about their employees' health is justified in light of the consequential intrusion into the employees' privacy.
- If any kind of medical testing (including drug/alcohol/genetic testing) is to be undertaken employers must ensure their employees are informed of the reason for the testing, the type of test, how the information obtained will be used and to whom it will be disclosed.
- Employers should note that generally the Information Commissioner considers that drug and alcohol testing should only be conducted for health and safety reasons.
- The Information Commissioner considers that genetic testing is only appropriate in very limited circumstances and should not be used to predict an employee's future general health.

---

1 Control of Substances Hazardous to Health Regulations 1999 (SI 1999/437), reg 11(3); Control of Lead at Work Regulations 2002 (SI 2002/2676), reg 10(5), Control of Asbestos at Work Regulations 2002 (SI 2002/2675), reg 21(1)(6) and Ionising Radiations Regulations 1999 (SI 1999/3232), reg 24(3).

Subject access requests

Lisa Mayhew

To employers and their advisers, subject access requests, or as they are more commonly known, access requests, represent the sharp end of data protection. An individual's right to gain access to information about them has been enhanced significantly following the implementation of s 7 of the Data Protection Act 1998 ('the DPA 1998'). Employers have found it difficult to respond to potentially far-reaching access requests and this has not been helped by the fact that the right has been misused in the context of employment litigation. The increasing number of disputes between employers and employees about access requests has resulted in an increasing number of the complaints received by the Information Commissioner involving allegations that individuals have been denied their right of subject access to personal data held about them, particularly in the form of emails.

This chapter will explain the statutory regime behind access requests and will consider the obligations on employees who make such requests and employers who receive them. It will also review the problems which commonly arise and will consider possible future developments, particularly in the light of ongoing government consultation on access requests and recent case law.

The basic right

The essence of DPA 1998, s 7 is that it provides an individual with a right of access to personal data, entitling him to know:
- whether a data controller is processing any of his personal data and, if so,
  o what it is;
  o its source (if known);
  o why it is being processed; and
  o to whom the data is or may be disclosed.

The Information Commissioner says in the Employment Practices Data Protection Code (the 'Code of Practice') that employees can exercise their access rights to be told what information their employers hold on them in the context of, for example, sickness records, disciplinary or training records, appraisals or performance review notes, emails, word processed documents, email logs, audit trails, information held in personnel files and interview notes.

Previously, under the Data Protection Act 1984, employees were only entitled to gain access to information contained in computerised records. However, the reach of DPA 1998, s 7 is far wider, as it extends to structured paper records, as well as those held on computer.

The Information Commissioner, along with others (such as the Campaign for Freedom of Information), trumpeted the new right and successfully publicised its existence. By way of example, the Information Commissioner ran two publicity campaigns featuring eye-catching headlines such as: 'Does someone want to see you fired?' and 'How far are you from being black-listed?'. Such headlines did little to take access requests out of a dispute context and succeeded in their aim of raising employee awareness of their access rights.

How do you make an access request?

DPA 1998, s 7(2) sets down a number of requirements for an access request to be legitimate. In short, they are that:
- a request must be in writing (although it does not need expressly to describe itself as being a request made under the DPA 1998);
- if required by the data controller, it must offer to pay a fee of up to a prescribed maximum (currently £10); and
- if reasonably required by the data controller, it must provide such information as is necessary in order for the data controller to satisfy itself as to the identity of the person making the request and also to locate the information which the person is seeking.

Common questions that arise following receipt of an access request

Has the request been addressed to the correct data controller?

Normally, the identity of the data controller will be obvious and, typically, it will be the employee's employing entity (or former employing entity). Where difficulties can arise is in the context of large organisations where there may be a number of associated group companies. In those situations, it may be that the employee has addressed his access request to a group company which does not control the processing of his personal data. How should the employer respond?

It would be tempting for an employer to respond to an access request that has been addressed to an incorrect data controller by undertaking a swift search for the employee's personal data and rapidly respond by saying that none is held. However, this could lead to more work for the employer down the line, because the employee may respond by serving numerous access requests addressed to all possible group companies, so that one of them will hit home. Such a tactic would require the group to undertake searches in response to each and every request. Therefore, a more practical way forward would be to notify the employee that he has named an incorrect data controller and tell him that unless he requests otherwise, a search will be undertaken of the data management systems controlled by his employing entity. From a practical perspective, as far as a search of emails is concerned, naming the correct data controller in the context of large corporations may not be so relevant if the technology systems (for example email servers) are shared by the various group companies.

Does the employer have to accept the fee?

No. It may be more trouble to process a £10 payment than it is worth. Therefore, it is open to an employer either to destroy a cheque or return the money to the employee.

When is it appropriate to ask for evidence of the identity of the person making the request?

Either when somebody else (for example a relative) is making a request on behalf of the individual concerned, or when the accidental disclosure of information to somebody who isn't the employee is likely to cause damage or distress to the employee. In the former case, it would be sensible to ask to see a copy of a letter of consent from the employee authorising the third party to obtain personal data on his behalf. Where there is a risk of the latter scenario, an employer could ask the individual making the request if he can confirm some personal information which is known to both parties and which it would be reasonable to expect the employee to know, or ask the person to produce a document that might reasonably be expected only to be in the employee's possession. Otherwise, the employer should rely on the usual signature of the individual as proof of identity and the information may be sent to an address known to the employer as being the address of the person making the request.

What if the scope of the request is so wide that it is difficult to know where to start?

DPA 1998, s 7(3) provides:

> Where a data controller reasonably requires further information ... to locate the information which that person seeks ... the data controller is not obliged to comply with the request unless he is supplied with that further information.

However, the key word here is 'reasonably'. If an employer is faced with a request for 'all personal data held on me' it will be reasonable for him to respond by asking for the request to be narrowed. For example, if the employee has requested that an email search be undertaken, the employer could ask him what categories of information he is looking for (for example decisions made about a disciplinary matter), the period of time during which they are likely to have been created and the names of the people who are likely to hold that information on email. Conversely, if the employee has already submitted a narrow and focused request, the risk is that the employer would be perceived as playing for time and being unreasonable in seeking further clarification of the request. Indeed, the Information Commissioner has stated that he will take a dim view of such conduct.

Can an access request be made on behalf of a dead person?

No. 'Personal data' means data relating to a *living* individual. Therefore, requests cannot be made on behalf of deceased employees.

Can data be amended or deleted following receipt of an access request?

Not with the intention of avoiding an employer's obligations under the DPA 1998. DPA 1998, s 8(6) provides:

> The information to be supplied pursuant to a request under section 7 must be supplied by reference to the data in question at the time when the request is received, except that it may take account of any amendment or deletion made between that time and the time when the information is supplied, being an amendment or deletion that would have been made regardless of the receipt of the request.

Therefore, only routine amendments or deletions can be made following receipt of an access request. It would be a breach of the DPA 1998 if any data were changed or deleted with the aim of holding back information prejudicial to the employer.

How to respond to an access request

DPA 1998, s 7 provides that in addition to being given a description of:

(i) the personal data;
(ii) the purposes for which it is being processed; and
(iii) to whom it may be disclosed,

the individual is also entitled:

> to have communicated to him in an intelligible form –
> (i) the information constituting any personal data of which that individual is the data subject, and
> (ii) any information available to the data controller as to the source of [that] data.

DPA 1998, s 8(2) goes on to state that the above obligation:

> must be complied with by supplying the data subject with a copy of the information in permanent form unless –
> (a) the supply of such a copy is not possible or would involve disproportionate effort, or
> (b) the data subject agrees otherwise.

Time limit for responding to an access request

DPA 1998, s 7(8) states that:

> ... a data controller shall comply with a request under this section promptly and in any event before the end of the prescribed period beginning with the relevant day.

The prescribed period is 40 days. The relevant day means the day upon which the employer receives the request or, if the employer has reasonably exercised his right under DPA 1998, s 7(3) and requested more information to narrow the request, then within 40 days of receipt of that additional information.

In order to minimise the prospects of criticism by the Information Commissioner, if an employer has had to ask for further information to narrow the request, but there is still other information which is straightforward to locate, then the employer should provide information about the more easily located material within the original 40 days and only take advantage of the second 40-day trigger point in respect of the information which is more difficult to locate.

Disproportionate effort

Provision of information in a permanent form

'Disproportionate effort' is not defined in the DPA 1998. As a concept, however, it is often the source of much disagreement between employers, employees and employment practitioners. First, the DPA 1998 makes it clear that the disproportionate effort provision is not something which an employer can rely on to justify a refusal to undertake a search for data. The wording of DPA 1998, s 8(2)(a) is clear in that the disproportionate effort concept is only a reason for not supplying a copy of data in permanent form, as opposed to not giving access to it at all.

Factors which the Information Commissioner says that he will take into account in determining whether the supply of information in permanent form amounts to disproportionate effort include:
- the cost of provision of the information;
- the length of time it may take to provide the information;
- how difficult or otherwise it may be for the data controller to provide the information; and
- the size of the organisation of which the request has been made.

The above factors will always be balanced against the effect on the employee of not receiving the data in a permanent form. It is therefore envisaged that other methods of providing the information contained in the personal data to the employee should be explored, such as loading computerised data onto a floppy disk, or even allowing the employee access to the employer's premises to inspect particular data.

Provision of information in an intelligible form

Before moving on to consider the appropriateness of the current disproportionate effort provision, it is worth also noting that the DPA 1998 obliges an employer to supply the information in an 'intelligible form' (as well as in a permanent form). Therefore, if the employer holds information in a coded form which cannot be understood without the key to the code then, assuming no other exemptions apply (see 'Exemptions' section below), the employer will need to supply the employee with whatever additional information is needed to make the information intelligible to him.

Resource intensive

Returning then to the disproportionate effort concept, it is something which has come in for a great deal of criticism from employers. This is because they (and their advisers) find it difficult to accept that an exercise which can be extremely resource-intensive and take many days to carry out (all at the employer's own expense) is justifiable. In short, employers complain that widely framed access requests place a disproportionately onerous burden on them, even when weighed against the benefit to be gained by the employee in receiving a full response to his request.

News of employers' discontent did reach the ears of the Information Commissioner, who published guidance in the context of requests for personal data contained in emails (see 'The problem with emails' below). The Information Commissioner implicitly recognised the difficulties faced by employers in responding to access requests when she (as the Information Commissioner then was) stated:

> In practice, however, the Commissioner might exercise her discretion and not seek to enforce a data subject's rights if she is satisfied that to give access would involve disproportionate effort on the part of the controller.

There seemed here to be some recognition by the Information Commissioner that the concept of proportionality may be taken into account by her in deciding whether or not to take enforcement action where there has been a breach at the stage of giving access to material (rather than just in relation to the form in which it is provided, as strictly required by the legislation). That said, the current Information Commissioner's support for embracing a wider concept of proportionality has, to date, been limited. His starting point remains as set out in Part 2 of the Code of Practice, which is that:

> Given the significance of employment records, an employer should only rely on the disproportionate effort exemption from providing a copy in exceptional circumstances.

The Bodil Lindqvist case

Irrespective of the narrow 'disproportionate effort' wording contained in the DPA 1998, it is likely that the overarching principle of proportionality in the context of access requests will be refined further over the coming months.

Proportionality is a general principle of Community law. It follows that EC Directive 95/46/EC on the protection of individuals with regard to the processing of personal data and the free movement of such data ('the Directive') and the national legislation implementing it must be interpreted and applied by the national courts in accordance with that overriding principle. A relevant question to ask when an onerous access request has been received is whether the benefit to be derived from it by the employee is disproportionate to the burden placed on the employer in responding to it.

There is support for the above view in the ECJ's decision in *Bodil Lindqvist* (Case C-101/01), [2003] All ER (D) 77 (Nov). In that case, Mrs Lindqvist had been charged with breach of the Swedish legislation on the protection of personal data for publishing on her home internet site personal data about a number of people who worked with her on a voluntary basis in a parish of the Swedish Protestant Church. Mrs Lindqvist described, in a mildly humorous manner, the jobs held by her colleagues and their hobbies. In many cases, family circumstances, telephone numbers and other matters were mentioned. She also stated that one colleague had injured her foot and was working half-time on medical grounds (being sensitive personal data). Mrs Lindqvist had not informed her colleagues of the existence of her internet pages or obtained their consent to publish these details about them. However, she removed the pages in question as soon as she became aware that they were not appreciated by some of her colleagues.

The Swedish courts had doubts as to the interpretation of the Directive and referred a number of questions to the ECJ. One of the questions was whether the provisions of the Directive could be regarded as bringing about a restriction which conflicts with the general principles of freedom of expression, or other freedoms and rights which are

applicable within the European Union and are enshrined in Art 10 of the European Convention on the Protection of Human Rights and Fundamental Freedoms. In answering that question, the ECJ said:

> ... the Directive quite properly includes rules with a degree of flexibility and, in many instances, leaves to the Member States the task of deciding the details or choosing between options ... thus, it is, rather, at the stage of the application at national level of the legislation implementing Directive 95/46 in individual cases that a balance must be found between the rights and interests involved ... Consequently it is for the authorities and courts of the Member States not only to interpret their national law in a manner consistent with Directive 95/46 but also to make sure they do not rely on an interpretation of it which would be in conflict with the fundamental rights protected by the Community legal order or with the other general principles of Community law, such as inter alia the principle of proportionality ... It is for the referring court to take account, in accordance with the principle of proportionality, of all the circumstances of the case before it, in particular, the duration of the breach of the rules implementing Directive 95/46 and the importance, for the persons concerned, of the protection of the data disclosed.

Following on from the remarks made in the *Lindqvist* case and those also made in the Court of Appeal's decision in *Durant* (see Chapter 1) it may be a legitimate argument for an employer to claim that the burden placed on it in searching for the data and providing a complete response to a wide access request is disproportionate to the employee's proprietary interest in receiving that data, particularly where the harm caused to the employee in not responding is not great.

Exemptions

The DPA 1998 contains a number of exemptions to the rights of individuals to access information about themselves, but they are not that easy to find as they are not all contained in one place. The exemptions available and their scope are explored in Chapter 8.

The exemptions which will usually be most relevant to employers in relation to subject access requests are contained in DPA 1998, Sch 7 which is entitled 'Miscellaneous Exemptions'. There are 11 miscellaneous exemptions in all, but four in particular crop up the most often. They are:

- confidential references;
- management forecasting or management planning;
- negotiations; and
- legal professional privilege.

Each is considered in more detail below.

Confidential references

Paragraph 1 of DPA 1998, Sch 7 says:

Personal data [is] exempt from section 7 if [it consists] of a reference given or to be given in confidence by the data controller for the purposes of:
(a) the education, training or employment, or prospective education, training or employment of the data subject,
(b) the appointment, or prospective appointment, of the data subject to any office, or
(c) the provision, or prospective provision, by the data subject of any service.

As a result, an employee cannot use DPA 1998, s 7 to obtain a copy from his employer (or, more likely, former employer) of the confidential reference which it gave to a prospective employer. However, this provision only applies to the data controller (that is, the giver of the reference) so an employee could use DPA 1998, s 7 to apply to the new employer (or potential employer) for a copy of the reference which it received. That said, disclosure of the reference would necessarily entail disclosure of its author's identity. Therefore, there are potential 'third party' rights under DPA 1998, s 7(4) which need to considered before disclosure can be given (see below for a discussion on third party information).

That said, because DPA 1998, s 7(4) only imposes limitations on disclosing information 'relating to another **individual** who can be identified from that information' the widespread view is that the third party exemption only applies in the context of references where the reference has been written by an individual (for example a line manager) as opposed to being a corporate reference (namely a standard factual account of the person's employment). However, if there is any doubt about this, the safest approach to take is not to disclose the reference without its author's consent.

Management forecasting or management planning

Paragraph 5 of DPA 1998, Sch 7 provides:

Personal data processed for the purposes of management forecasting or management planning to assist the data controller in the conduct of any business or other activity [is] exempt from the subject information provisions in any case to the extent to which the application of those provisions would be likely to prejudice the conduct of that business or other activity.

Therefore, employees cannot use DPA 1998, s 7 to gain access to certain data if their employer is carrying out a redundancy exercise, or a succession planning exercise, or a pay review or is proposing a company takeover. However, the second 'likely to prejudice' part of the exemption cannot be ignored, which means that the management forecasting or planning exercises need to be ongoing. So, once a redundancy programme or a recruitment exercise has been completed, it would be open to an employee to serve an access request on his employer and seek disclosure of data concerning him which was created during the redundancy or recruitment exercise.

Negotiations

Paragraph 7 of DPA 1998, Sch 7 provides:

Personal data which consist[s] of records of the intentions of the data controller in relation to any negotiations with the data subject [is] exempt from the subject information provisions in any case to the extent to which the application of those provisions would be likely to prejudice those negotiations.

Therefore, where an employer is negotiating with an employee (for example over pay or the settlement of an employment claim), the employee is not entitled to gain access to information about the employer's intentions in those negotiations, if such access would prejudice the negotiations.

An obvious example would be if an employer had reserved an amount for settlement of a claim in its annual budget, which, if known to the employee, would reveal the employer's settlement strategy. However, it is important to note that this exemption only applies to data going to the employer's intentions in the settlement discussions and not to any other background data concerning the employee's claim. In other words, just because an employee is bringing a claim against his employer which, at the same time, it is negotiating to settle, does not justify a blanket refusal by the employer to disclose any information at all in response to an access request.

Legal professional privilege

Paragraph 10 of DPA 1998, Sch 7 says:

Personal data [is] exempt from the subject information provisions if the data consists of information in respect of which a claim to legal professional privilege (or, in Scotland, to confidentiality of communications) could be maintained in legal proceedings.

Legal professional privilege does not have a special meaning in the context of the DPA 1998. The same approach should be taken as in other contexts when assessing if a document is subject to legal professional privilege. Briefly, information has legal professional privilege attached to it if it is contained in a confidential communication passing between the employer and his legal adviser (which could be an in-house lawyer) for the dominant purpose of giving or receiving legal advice.

Third party information

As we have seen, the DPA 1998 is all about balancing the rights and interests of others. At its core is the balance between an employee's right to access personal information relating to him and the employer's need to process information about its employees. However, given that a large proportion of information about a particular employee will also contain data about other employees, the rights of those third party employees to privacy also deserve protection. This is expressly recognised in DPA 1998, s 7(4), which states:

Where a data controller cannot comply with the request without disclosing information relating to another individual who can be identified from that information, he is not obliged to comply with the request unless:
(a) the other individual has consented to the disclosure of the information to the person making the request, or
(b) it is reasonable in all the circumstances to comply with the request without the consent of the other individual.

The first point to note here is that by its very definition, 'disclosure' means revealing information to an employee for the first time. Therefore, a written appraisal conducted by an employee's line manager is unlikely to be caught by the DPA 1998, s 7(4) 'third party exemption' as the employee, by virtue of being present at the appraisal, will already know the identity of the person passing comment on him. As a result, the third party exemption only kicks in when information relating to third parties has not previously been seen by the employee.

The second point to note about the third party exemption is that it only arises if it is part of the personal data of the employee making the request. Given the Court of Appeal's recent narrow interpretation of the meaning of personal data in the *Durant* case (for which see Chapter 1) the majority of third party information will not form part of the employee's own personal data. Therefore, if information about another person is not part of the personal data sought, then no question of a DPA 1998, s 7(4) balancing exercise arises at all.

In situations where third party information does form part of an employee's personal data, the employer will need to weigh up the competing interests of the third parties who have a right to privacy against the employee's right to gain access to his particular personal data.

There will be no issue in disclosing the third party information if the third party has consented to its disclosure, but there is no positive obligation contained in the DPA 1998 to seek that consent. However, where consent has not been given (for example where it has not been sought or it has been refused), the employer is still required by DPA 1998, s 7(4) to comply with the access request and disclose third party information, if it is reasonable in all the circumstances to do so. To avoid falling foul not only of the legislation but other legal obligations (such as confidentiality), disclosure without consent should not be made until proper consideration has been given to all of the relevant factors. DPA 1998, s 7(6) highlights some of the factors to be taken into account in deciding this, but the list is not exhaustive. They are:

(a) any duty of confidentiality owed to the other individual,
(b) any steps taken by the data controller with a view to seeking the consent of the other individual,
(c) whether the other individual is capable of giving consent, and
(d) any express refusal of consent by the other individual.

The fact that the same information has previously been provided to the employee will be relevant in assessing reasonableness, as will the fact that particular information is generally publicly available.

Example: The employer's records detailing the employee's claim for a benefit include the name of the manager dealing with the claim. The manager had provided his name on an earlier occasion when he met the employee at interview to complete the claim forms. The employer would not be justified in withholding the manager's name in those circumstances. It follows that an employer is less likely to be able to justify withholding the information where the third party is a member of staff acting in the course of his duties rather than an individual acting in a private capacity.

Example: Two senior managers speculate in email correspondence with each other about the reasons why one of their employees failed to attend a weekend business function. They speculate that this might be because the employee had to care for her children. In this scenario, the safest course of action would be to seek the two managers' consent for the email traffic to be disclosed and, in the absence of this, consider whether their names could be redacted in such a way as to protect their identity before disclosure is given. If the managers do not consent to disclosure and a redaction exercise would not protect their identities, the safest course of action to take would be not to disclose. Ultimately, if the employer's actions come to be scrutinised by the Information Commissioner or a court and a conclusion is drawn that the email traffic should be disclosed, then this will be an answer to any complaint by the managers that their rights to confidentiality have been broken.

The third party exemption remains a problematic area for employers to grapple with. There is little guidance on the matter, and indeed Auld LJ in the *Durant* case said:

I believe that the courts should be wary of attempting to devise any principles of general application one way or the other ... much will depend, on the one hand, on the criticality of the third party information forming part of the data subject's personal data to the legitimate protection of his privacy, and, on the other, to the existence or otherwise of any obligation of confidence to the third party or any other sensitivity of the third party disclosure sought.

Developing an infrastructure to respond to access requests

Good practice dictates (and the Information Commissioner expressly recommends) that employers establish and follow a policy for dealing with access requests.

In the interests of certainty and even-handedness, it is recommended that an employer's written policy for responding to access requests contains a number of consistent starting points, for example, that a maximum number of email accounts will be searched. Assuming these are carefully thought out and can be justified, this has the advantage of establishing a proportionate bedrock to the policy which is known to those who will be responsible for operating it. It is also recommended that any policy retains elements of flexibility, recognising that access requests will differ in nature. By way of illustration, if a policy contained certain limitations around a search (such as the maximum number of email accounts) there should be an opportunity for an employee to seek to justify a different or extended search, but only on *Durant* grounds. (For a detailed discussion on *Durant* see Chapter 1.) In other words, if the employee can justify a different or extended search on the basis that this is necessary to check (and, if necessary, correct) information about him which goes to his right of privacy, then there should be scope for accommodating this.

It will be for each employer to determine what policy is appropriate within its particular organisation. For example, the available technology will have a huge impact on what email searches may be undertaken. Other available resources (such as human resources, information technology and legal departments) will also be influential factors.

Experience shows that it is essential that all parties who will be responsible for devising and implementing an access request response policy work together. Typically, this will involve liaison between legal, human resources and information technology departments. What is critical, however, is that an overall co-ordinator for the company (or, if more appropriate, a particular business unit) is nominated to be responsible for responding to access requests.

Access request response policy checklist

As varied as individual employers' access request policies might be, there are a number of key aspects which should be incorporated into all of them:

- an audit should be undertaken of the systems used by a company to hold and process information about employees. A spreadsheet could usefully be compiled in the form of Appendix C detailing the potential sources for data;

- whenever an access request has been received, checks should be carried out to establish whether it has been properly made. For example, has the request been made in writing, has it been addressed to the correct data controller? If the employer requires a fee, has the correct fee been submitted? Crucially, has sufficient information been provided to enable the employer to locate the data sought?

- if the access request is defective in any way, there should be a standard form letter to send to the employee aimed at correcting any defects. An example of such a letter is contained at Appendix D;

- where an individual has previously made an access request with which the employer has complied, there should be scope for checking whether there has been a 'reasonable interval' before the company has to comply with another request from that same individual (see section on 'Repeat requests' below for a discussion on this point);

- consideration should be given to whether the access request has been served as a tactical litigation weapon (see 'Access request used in the context of litigation' below for discussion on this). A prudent employer would seek legal advice on this issue, because the validity of its approach to the response will stand or fall on whatever decision it makes on this point;

- once an access request has been framed correctly, there should be a system in place for undertaking the relevant searches and keeping a record of their results. This should be done within the relevant 40-day time limit and a spreadsheet kept along the lines of Appendix E;

- once the searches have been completed, the co-ordinator responsible for the access request should review the documentation received to check whether it falls within any of the exemptions. Any information which falls within an exemption should not be disclosed;

Information which is held back because a decision has been taken that an exemption applies is not something which the employee making the access request (or their adviser) is entitled to see. He is also not entitled to know that information has been held back, or why it has been held back. However, in case the information held back becomes the subject of scrutiny by the Information Commissioner or the court, copies of the material held back should be stored safely and detailed records kept, explaining the reasons why the material was withheld. This will stand an employer in good stead, should its reasoning subsequently be challenged.

- where a search for personal data returns a very large number of documents/emails, the co-ordinator should consider if the provision of copies would involve a disproportionate effort (see 'Disproportionate effort' above). Flexible parameters could be set beyond which the employer would not normally provide copies (say 500 emails), unless the employee could justify disclosure on *Durant* grounds (for example where there have been lots of health records compiled in an ill-health case which the employee wants to check are accurate);
- once the relevant information has been collated and sifted to remove any exempt information, an employer should have a template letter available to respond to the access request, usually enclosing copies of the relevant data and providing the employee with the information set out in the 'Basic right' section at the beginning of this chapter. A sample response to an access request is set out at Appendix F.

In order to operate a policy along the lines described above, an employer (again, depending on its size and resources) would be expected either to train the in-house personnel who will be responsible for implementing the policy, or to seek external legal advice to assist in lawful compliance with its obligations.

A useful tip to assist employers in responding to access requests is to ask the employee at the beginning whether he wishes to see copies of any personal data which he has already seen. If the answer is no, then this can serve to cut down significantly on the material which needs to be disclosed to him, as it would exclude, for example, emails to or from the employee which he would clearly have seen before.

The problem with emails

How far do you need to search?

Experience has shown that emails represent fertile territory for access requests. Employees who were (or still are) regular users of their employer's email system know that it can be used to record personal information about people. They are also aware that it is very difficult permanently to destroy data held on the email system, so it is likely that there will be a high volume of data about them going back over some time. However, from an employer's perspective, a wide search of its email systems can prove extremely resource intensive in terms of both time and cost. In particular, it may be expensive to retrieve deleted emails, especially where this may require the rebuilding of large computer archives, rather than the retrieval of small amounts of data.

The tensions between employers and employees in relation to email searches are something of which the Information Commissioner is aware. In an attempt to assist matters, the Information Commissioner produced: 'subject access & emails' guidelines in 2000[1]. Those guidelines make it clear that the access request should be one requesting personal data as defined by the DPA 1998 (and as subsequently interpreted in the *Durant* case – see Chapter 1) and should provide enough information to assist the employer to locate the information (such as the names of the authors and recipients of the emails and the date range and subject of the emails). However, even if the basics of an access request exist, the guidance states:

> [enforcement] notices are not served automatically, however, and in deciding whether it is proper in particular cases to serve a notice, the Commissioner will take a number of factors into account ... if the Commissioner considers that the controller can locate the data but has

not provided a copy to the data subject then she will be more inclined to recommend enforcement.

Subject to all other requirements of the legislation as detailed in this chapter being met, where personal data is contained in live emails, the Information Commissioner (and probably a court) will be inclined to take enforcement action where the employer has not provided copies of the information sought.

On the issue of emails which are not held on live systems, but exist in archive or back-up form, the Information Commissioner says:

> In practice, however, the Commissioner might exercise her discretion and not seek to enforce a data subject's rights if she is satisfied that to give access would involve disproportionate effort on the part of the controller. In forming a judgment as to whether the effort involved would be disproportionate, she will consider:
> - What is the nature of the data and the likely effect on the individual if the data [is or is] not retrieved? The more serious, the more likely it will be that the Commissioner will take action.
> - What is the controller's policy in relation to archive or other 'non-live' data? If it is to retrieve data only in exceptional circumstances (eg serious criminal allegations) then it may be disproportionate to have to retrieve the data in response to a request from a data subject who only wants a copy out of interest. In attempting to determine what a data controller's policy is, the Commissioner may request sight of policy documents and/or an account of the practices followed by the controller in the past.
> - How hard would it be for the controller to retrieve the data? Is it possible to retrieve small amounts of data or is it necessary to reconstitute large computer archives? How much will it cost?
> - In the case of back-up data is there any evidence to suppose that this version differs materially from that held on the live system?

To summarise, the Commissioner's approach is that where emails are held on live systems and can be located, she will seek to enforce subject access if this has been denied. Where data [is] held elsewhere, the Commissioner will weigh the interests of the data subject against the effort that the controller would have to take to recover the data and in many instances may be likely to decide not to take action

Are personal emails disclosable?

The vast majority of employers accept that where employees are given access to an email system they will, from time to time, use it to send and receive personal emails, as well as business-related ones. In the early days of the DPA 1998, a common question was whether an employer was a data controller for personal emails held on its system. The Information Commissioner's view on this is clear, in that employers will usually be the data controller for **all** emails held on their system. The reason given is:

> This is because they [that is the employer] will keep at least some control over how and why messages are processed, for example by restricting the purposes for which workers can send personal emails or by retaining or monitoring personal emails to ensure the security of their systems.

The main issue to bear in mind here is that referred to above in relation to third party information, which is that if an email was written in a private rather than an official capacity, then it is likely that only exceptional circumstances will justify disclosure of third party information without the consent of the individual concerned.

Should an employer tell other employees that their email accounts are being searched to respond to an access request?

There are no hard and fast rules about this, but it is suggested that where an employer does not have an email policy which is known to employees and expressly states that an employee's emails may be accessed and searched for the purposes of responding to access requests, then the employer should tell the employee before the search is undertaken that it will be searching his email accounts to respond to an access request. However, it should only be a matter of informing the employee of the search, rather than asking for his consent. This is because, in accordance with DPA 1998, Sch 2, the processing is necessary for compliance with a legal obligation. If an employer does not have a clear policy enabling it to search email accounts to respond to access requests and does not tell an employee that it intends searching his email accounts, the risk is that the third party employee may have a claim for breach of the implied obligation of trust and confidence. However, the likelihood of such a claim being brought in reality is questionable.

Territorial jurisdiction of the DPA 1998

The issue of the territorial application of the DPA 1998 arises most often in the context of access requests served on international employers where employees demand access to information held on them overseas. The obvious example is email. Can an employee demand access to information contained in emails where those emails originate from an overseas colleague's email account (for example a colleague based in America)?

The territorial application of the DPA 1998 is covered in Chapter 1.

Repeat requests

DPA 1998, s 8(3) says:

> Where a data controller has previously complied with a request made under section 7 by an individual, the data controller is not obliged to comply with a subsequent identical or similar request under that section by that individual unless a reasonable interval has elapsed between compliance with the previous request and the making of the current request.

The DPA 1998 does not give any guidance on what would amount to a 'reasonable interval'. This will therefore depend on the facts of each case.

In order to achieve workable parameters in an employer's access request policy, an employer could specify that if a similar or identical request is made within, say, six months of the previous request this will not constitute a 'reasonable interval'. The policy could go on to state that if the employer receives a second request from an employee within six months, it will put the onus on the employee by asking him to justify why he believes a 'reasonable interval' has lapsed since his initial request.

Enforcement

What can an employee do if he believes that his access request has not been complied with properly?

In short, there are two avenues which an employee can go down to seek enforcement of his access request. They are:
- the Information Commissioner – to seek an enforcement notice compelling a proper response;
- the court – for an order under DPA 1998, s 7(9) compelling a proper response.

The reason why employees can pursue enforcement action (described in more general terms in the 'Enforcement' section of Chapter 1) is because the sixth data protection principle provides that personal data must be: 'processed in line with data subjects' rights'. Those rights include the right to serve an access request on their employer, so a breach of that right could lead to enforcement action being taken.

Information Commissioner versus going to court

The attractions of complaining to the Information Commissioner before launching court proceedings are:
- there is no cost involved for the employee;

- the case will be assessed by somebody who is an expert in data protection issues; and
- irrespective of the Information Commissioner's view on enforcement, the employee could still subsequently pursue court action as well.

If an employee pursues court action before complaining to the Information Commissioner, then in the absence of compelling reasons for doing so (such as the need for urgent correction of inaccurate data) it would be open to the employer to argue that court action was premature (and therefore an abuse of process) as there is an alternative avenue available for rectification (namely the Information Commissioner).

Another reason for thinking carefully before complaining to the court, is that the losing party is likely to be ordered to contribute to the winning party's legal costs. Therefore, most employees think carefully before using this remedy, so as not to risk a bill of several thousands of pounds should they lose.

The court's discretion

In the same way that the Information Commissioner's enforcement powers are discretionary, the DPA 1998 also confers a discretion on the courts as to whether or not to grant a remedy in the context of access requests. This discretion is contained in DPA 1998, s 7(9) which provides:

> If a court is satisfied on the application of any person who has made a request under the foregoing provisions of this section that the data controller in question has failed to comply with the request in contravention of those provisions, the court may order him to comply with the request.

The key word denoting the court's discretion is 'may'. However, as Auld LJ confirmed in the *Durant* decision (para 74 of the judgment), the discretion conferred by DPA 1998, s 7(9) is 'general and untrammelled'. Therefore, it will be open to the court in any particular case where there has been a breach of the access request requirements to decide whether to decline or award a remedy.

Damages

As we have seen in Chapter 1, if an employee is going to obtain an award of damages from the court under DPA 1998, s 13, he needs to be able to show more than pure distress – he also needs to demonstrate that he has suffered loss as a result of the breach. Therefore, in the context of access requests, it is unlikely that an employee will be able to mount a successful claim for damages, as it will be rare for an employee to be able to show that he has suffered financial loss as a result of the access request not being complied with properly. The more common remedy in the courts will be an order compelling compliance with the access request.

Access request used in the context of litigation

As the level of awareness of rights under the DPA 1998 has continued to grow, so has the number of access requests received by employers in the context of employment litigation. Their proliferation has been driven by the notion that the purpose behind the request is immaterial. The DPA 1998 does not talk about requests having to be made in good faith and so an employee's motivation has until now seemed irrelevant. As a consequence, access requests have been used to obtain pre-action disclosure and to create as much work as possible for the employer, with the aim being to pressurise them into offering a higher settlement than they might otherwise have done. However, the *Durant* case may change matters.

Pre-action disclosure

The reason why access requests have until now proved to be an effective weapon in obtaining disclosure of documents in a litigation context is because they have four potential advantages over the standard litigation disclosure process. These are:

- they can be served on the employer at a far earlier stage – for example prior to issuing employment tribunal proceedings and prior to reaching the disclosure stage in employment litigation;
- litigation disclosure only covers information which is relevant to the issues in dispute, whereas

access requests are not constrained in this way (although they are limited to documents containing personal data);

- the litigation disclosure process operates to prevent a party going on a 'fishing expedition', namely a speculative mission to find out what documents are in the other party's possession. Again, there has previously been thought to be no such constraint in relation to access requests;

- in the litigation disclosure context, an employer is obliged to make a 'reasonable search' for relevant documents. What is 'reasonable' will depend on a number of factors, such as the number of documents, the nature and complexity of the proceedings, the ease and expense of retrieval of any particular document and the significance of any document which is likely to be located by the exercise. In contrast, arguably greater effort is required under the access request regime, because an employee is entitled to a copy of personal data, which must be supplied in a permanent form, unless the provision of a copy is impossible or involves 'disproportionate effort' (see above for a more detailed consideration of this).

Importance of the Durant case

The *Durant* case gave the Court of Appeal its first real opportunity to consider the scope and use of access requests in the context of litigation. The leading judgment of Auld LJ drew a number of conclusions which go some way towards supporting employers in refusing to answer access requests which have been motivated by an employee's desire to improve his litigation prospects.

First, Auld LJ began by noting that:

> The primary objective of the 1995 Directive is to protect individuals' fundamental rights, notably the right to privacy and accuracy of their personal data held by others (data controllers) in computerised form or similarly organised manual filing systems ...

As noted in Chapter 1, the context for Mr Durant's access request was litigation.

In a leading conclusion formed by Auld LJ, he said:

> ... the purpose of section 7 in entitling an individual to have access to information in the form of his 'personal data' is to enable him to check whether the data controller's processing of it unlawfully infringes his privacy and, if so, to take such steps as the Act provides, for example in sections 10 to 14, to protect it. It is not an automatic key to any information, readily accessible or not, of matters in which he may be named or involved. Nor is it to assist him, for example, to obtain discovery of documents that may assist him in litigation or complaints against third parties.

It is therefore suggested that the courts are unlikely to exercise their discretion to enforce access requests which are motivated by employment litigation, rather than a genuine desire to check the accuracy of information held on employees which goes to their right to privacy.

It will be a difficult decision for an employer to make on receipt of an access request whether it has been made in the context of litigation. However, to assist an employer in reaching its decision, it is recommended that the employer considers the timing of the request (for example, has it been served shortly before or after employment proceedings have been launched?) and the coincidence of issues covered in the request and the litigation (so, are they essentially about the same issues, rather than an employee's right to privacy?).

In the post-*Durant* era, employees and their advisers should think carefully before issuing court proceedings for a failure to respond to access requests. In the words of Buxton LJ at para 81 of the Court of Appeal's decision in *Durant*:

> In future, those contemplating such proceedings and those advising them must carefully scrutinise the guidance given in [this judgment] before going any further. That process should prevent the wholly unjustifiable burden and expense that has been imposed on the data controller in this case.

The case of PUK v David Wozencroft

The issue of access requests being deployed in the context of litigation was also examined by the Family Division of the High Court of Justice in the case of *PUK v David Wozencroft* [2002] EWHC 1724 (Fam). The facts of that case were that Dr Wozencroft had written a report about Mr P and his relationship with his daughter in the context of Mr P's application for a residence order in relation to his daughter, who now lived with his ex-wife. Following court proceedings, Mr P's application for a residence order was refused, largely because of the content of Dr Wozencroft's scathing report about him. Having lost those proceedings, Mr P then served an access request on Dr Wozencroft requesting copies of all documents accessible to Mr P under the DPA 1998. The reason for the request was because Mr P considered the content of Dr Wozencroft's report to be inaccurate and, therefore, he wanted to take corrective action under DPA 1998, s 14 (see 'Actions against inaccurate data' in Chapter 1). The distinction with *Durant* is that, whereas that case was about using an access request as a tactical pre-litigation disclosure exercise, here Mr P was seeking disclosure after litigation had occurred (and disclosure had therefore taken place). In this situation, Wilson J commented:

> ... in the exercise of the discretion the existence of a more appropriate forum for the articulation of these issues would be a decisive factor ... I say with confidence that it is an abuse of process to use later proceedings in order to ventilate challenges which were clearly apt to be ventilated in earlier proceedings.

Potential future developments

In October 2002, the Government initiated a formal consultation seeking views on the current access request arrangements. The Government has indicated that:

> ... the right of subject access must remain one of the central pillars of the UK's data protection regime ... the purpose of the review is solely to assess whether the practical arrangements made by the 1998 Act for the exercise of the right continue to operate satisfactorily or whether any 'running' adjustments are needed to take account of legal and technological changes.

The deadline for submitting views to the Government expired on 31 January 2003. However, as at the date of this Report, no steps had been taken to implement any recommendations. Potential changes include:

1. The £10 fee may either be abolished entirely or increased to reflect the administrative burden on the employer. This is because it is widely acknowledged that the cost of processing the fee will normally exceed the fee itself. Consideration may also be given to a multi-tier fee, so that, for example, an employee who requires a copy of his personnel file may be required to pay a more modest fee than an employee who requires an extensive search for his personal data.

2. The 40-day response time limit may be changed, perhaps to provide for a shorter time for providing readily available data and a longer time for providing data which is less readily available.

3. There may be a fixed period within which repeat applications will not be accepted, or a full-cost recovery fee can be charged.

4. Clear guidance (with examples) for employers in responding to access requests may be published.

5. A new provision may be added to the DPA 1998 entitling employees to know when information has been withheld from them and on what grounds.

6. More detailed guidance may be published on the meaning of some of the more difficult exemptions, such as management forecasting and negotiations.

Subject access requests — summary of main issues

- Every employee has a right to request access to his personal data.
- To be valid, an access request must satisfy the conditions set out in DPA 1998, s 7(2).
- The concept of disproportionate effort is problematic and does not provide employers with an excuse to refuse to comply with an access request.
- A key feature of the right to access personal data is that enforcement of the right is discretionary. It is likely that both the purpose of the request and the principle of proportionality will be taken into account in deciding whether to enforce.
- There are a number of exemptions from the right to access personal data.
- Care has to be taken in responding to access requests to ensure that data protection obligations to third parties (that is, anyone other than the person making the request) are not breached.
- Emails present another practical difficulty in dealing with access requests. How extensive does the search have to be?
- It is sensible for employers to put in place a policy to ensure consistency of approach to access requests.

Monitoring in the workplace

John Keith

An area which raises numerous data protection issues is that of monitoring in the workplace. This chapter will look at the extent to which employers can monitor their employees and the extent to which any information obtained as a result is admissible as evidence in a court or tribunal. We will also review the applicable legal principles of the Data Protection Act 1998 ('the DPA 1998'); the Human Rights Act 1998 ('the HRA 1998'), the Regulation of Investigatory Powers Act 2000 ('RIPA 2000') and the Telecommunications (Lawful Business Practice) (Interception of Communications) Regulations 2000 (SI 2000/2699) (the 'Lawful Business Practice Regulations').

Why monitor?

There are many reasons why an employer might want to monitor its employees and/or general members of the public and in certain circumstances may even feel obliged to do so. These include:

- to avoid harassment or other inappropriate behaviour by employees, particularly as this can leave the employer being vicariously liable for such actions;
- to monitor employees' performance and for training purposes (for example, monitoring of telephone calls to call centres);
- to prevent theft by employees;
- to control transmission of trade secrets and confidential information;
- to prevent ex-employees from soliciting current employees or customers.

The need for an employer to consider the purpose of monitoring is vital, given the many types of monitoring that can be carried out, each of which poses risks if carried out inappropriately. The options include:

- CCTV;
- audio bugging;
- vehicle/mobile telephone tracking;
- keyboard, email and internet monitoring;
- telephone monitoring;
- physical monitoring, including drugs and alcohol testing and searches;

- biometric tests, including finger-printing, hand geometry, iris scanning, voice recognition and automated face recognition.

The different kinds of monitoring will each pose different issues for an employer to consider, such as the extent to which the monitoring is invasive of employees' privacy; the extent to which the data obtained is accurate; and the extent to which the information obtained can be kept securely.

Is it legal?

Employers should consider the following sources and guidance when considering the legality of monitoring for the purposes of the DPA 1998:

- the DPA 1998 itself, particularly the data protection principles at DPA 1998, Sch 1, together with the requirements for processing data contained in DPA 1998, Sch 2 (relating to personal data) and DPA 1998, Sch 3 (relating to sensitive personal data), which are discussed below;
- case law interpreting the DPA 1998, particularly the case of *Durant v Financial Services Authority* [2003] EWCA Civ 1746, [2003] All ER (D) 124 (Dec), discussed briefly below and in more detail in Chapter 1; and
- the Employment Practices Data Protection Code (the 'Code of Practice'), Part 3, which deals with monitoring at work, together with supplementary guidance and separate guidance for small businesses, all of which can be found on the Information Commissioner's website: www.informationcommissioner.gov.uk.

Back to basics – looking at the DPA 1998 itself

Is the form of monitoring actually covered under the DPA 1998?

One preliminary point to consider is whether the monitoring proposed to be carried out actually falls within the DPA 1998 at all. The recent *Durant* case highlighted that to be covered by the provisions of the DPA 1998, non-computerised information must be held in a 'relevant filing system' and the information must be 'personal data'. The ambit of both of these aspects was held to be substantially narrower than was previously thought. The Information Commissioner has given guidance on the case which can be found on the Information Commissioner's website and is discussed in Chapter 1.

The *Durant* case will impact on monitoring as follows:
- monitoring carried out manually may fall outside the DPA 1998 altogether depending on how the results are to be stored, although the employer would still be subject to other legislation such as the HRA 1998;
- as a substantial amount of what might otherwise be thought to be personal data in fact falls outside the DPA 1998, for an employer who has been carrying out monitoring and subsequently receives a subject access request, the burden of responding may be substantially reduced; and
- employers who use only basic CCTV systems (for example, which use cameras which cannot be moved remotely and only record whatever the camera happens to pick up) may not be covered by the DPA 1998. The Information Commissioner has given further guidance on this issue which is available on the website referred to above.

Example: A company has swipe card entry to its premises with each employee having his own individualised pass card. Unknown to the employees, as well as providing entry to the premises, the technology can produce a list of entry times for each employee which the company uses on occasions in disciplinary proceedings. On the *Durant* criteria, the information would amount to personal data as the individual is the focus of any list of entry times and, as the information relates to the movement of individuals, it relates to their privacy.

Example: A company decides to search an employee's emails in the course of an investigation into alleged misconduct. The majority of these emails fall under three headings: correspondence with the employee's clients regarding the company's transactions with which he is involved; a small number of emails in which he has forwarded jokes to colleagues; and finally, emails to a colleague in which he asks his opinions on the merits of Grimsby Town Football Club. Which emails, if any, amount to personal data?

The answer is that none of them may amount to personal data. Correspondence with the client which does not have the employee as its focus, but rather relates to the company's transactions with which he is involved, would be excluded. The emails in which he has forwarded jokes may contain no information about the employee, other than the fact that he has forwarded the joke itself, and could not amount to biographical data in the *Durant* sense. Finally, the emails in which he is asking for the colleague's opinions on the football club are unlikely to amount to personal data unless he expresses opinions himself which may provide information as to his hobbies.

The *Durant* case could be seen as specific to its facts and, whilst a Court of Appeal decision, the interpretation of what amounts to 'personal data' may be open to subsequent challenge on the basis of European case law, which places great emphasis on the right to privacy, particularly in relation to health data.

Monitoring and 'processing' of personal data under the DPA 1998

Assuming that the information obtained through monitoring is personal data and is computerised or kept in a 'relevant filing system', monitoring is likely to fall within the definition of 'processing' under the DPA 1998, s 1.

Type of data and purpose of processing

The next issues for an employer to consider are the type of personal data which has been processed, that is whether information amounts to 'personal data' or 'sensitive personal data' (see Chapter 1), and the purpose for which the data is being processed.

The following sections will consider the data protection principles and how they impact on monitoring.

The data protection principles

Identifying the type of personal data being processed and the reason for such processing is the key to lawful monitoring, not least so as to comply with the first data protection principle in DPA 1998, Sch 1, namely:

> Personal data shall be processed fairly and lawfully and, in particular, shall not be processed unless –
> (a) at least one of the conditions in Schedule 2 is met, and
> (b) in case of sensitive personal data, at least one of the conditions in Schedule 3 is also met.

Conditions in DPA 1998, Sch 2 which may be relevant to an employer carrying out monitoring include DPA 1998, Sch 2 condition 2:

> The processing is necessary –
> (a) for the performance of a contract to which the data subject is a party, or
> (b) for the taking of steps at the request of the data subject with a view to entering into a contract.

DPA 1998, Sch 2 condition 3:

> The processing is necessary for compliance with any legal obligation to which the data controller is subject other than an obligation imposed by a contract.

or DPA 1998, Sch 2 condition 6(1):

> The processing is necessary for the purposes of legitimate interests pursued by the data controller or by the third party or parties to whom the data [is] disclosed, except where the processing is unwarranted in any particular case by reason of prejudice to the rights and freedoms or legitimate interests of the data subject.

DPA 1998, Sch 2 condition 2 will be relevant to obligations such as processing payroll information in order to pay an employee. DPA 1998, Sch 2 condition 3 is particularly relevant to obligations such as those on the employer to prevent discrimination in the workplace. DPA 1998, Sch 2 condition 6(1) introduces the concepts of proportionality and necessity, which are key to the Information Commissioner's concept of an 'impact assessment', which is discussed in greater detail in the section 'The Information Commissioner's Code of Practice' below.

The requirement for data to be processed fairly is what obliges employers to notify employees that data is being processed about them and is why covert monitoring is so difficult to justify from a legal perspective. One of the few ways that covert monitoring may be justified at all is because there is an important exemption (DPA 1998, s 29) relating to the first principle (DPA 1998, Sch 1) where processing is for the prevention or detection of crime or for the apprehension or prosecution of offenders. That is the basis for the statement by the Information Commissioner that covert monitoring will only be justified in circumstances where a criminal activity or something analogous is suspected.

A final condition which may be relevant is consent. The DPA 1998, Sch 2 condition states that:

> The data subject has given consent to the processing.

whilst the requirement of DPA 1998, Sch 3 is that:

> The data subject has given his explicit consent to the processing of the personal data.

The issue of consent is discussed in greater detail in Chapter 1. Suffice it to say here that in his Code of Practice, the Information Commissioner has decided that any consent must be 'freely given' and that he does not expect consent to be the condition usually relied upon to justify processing.

The other seven data protection principles are discussed in detail in Chapter 1. The aspects which relate particularly to monitoring are discussed below:
- **the third data protection principle (DPA 1998, Sch 1)** requires that personal data should be

adequate, relevant and not excessive in relation to the purposes for which it is processed.

> **Example:** An employer suspects that its employees are spending too much time sending and receiving emails of a private nature. It decides to open all emails on the basis that it has an explicit policy in which it reserves the right to do so.
>
> Regardless of any policy, such monitoring will be in breach of the third data protection principle (DPA 1998, Sch 1), as there are other ways of checking email use without reading the contents of each email, for example, 'call loggers' showing frequency of emails sent and the recipients of those emails.

- **The fourth data protection principle (DPA 1998, Sch 1)** requires that personal data is accurate and, where necessary, kept up to date.

> **Example:** An example of the impact of this principle on monitoring will be in the context of CCTV monitoring. An employer will need to ensure that the machinery and any tapes used to record images are of a high quality. If digital enhancing is required there will need to be a procedure to ensure the accuracy of that enhancement. If a recording system features technology such as time and location references these must be checked for accuracy.

- **The seventh data protection principle (DPA 1998, Sch 1)** requires appropriate technical and organisational measures to be taken against unauthorised and unlawful processing of personal data.

> **Example:** CCTV monitoring may unintentionally capture images of members of the public. In these circumstances, staff operating CCTV should be adequately trained not to misuse the technology. This example is also relevant to compliance with other data protection principles, including the first and second data protection principles (DPA 1998, Sch 1) which are discussed in further detail in Chapter 1. The need for security is also discussed in further detail in the section 'Security of data obtained through monitoring' below.

The Information Commissioner's Code of Practice

The Code of Practice does not have the status of law, but is an expression of the Information Commissioner's view as to how to achieve compliance with the DPA 1998. It is not the only way of complying, but if an employer has followed the guidance set out in the Code of Practice it will minimise the risk of successful enforcement proceedings.

What is monitoring?

The Code of Practice issued by the Information Commissioner gives a very broad definition of monitoring, but qualifies this by saying that the definition is not a 'hard and fast' one:

> Monitoring means activities that set out to collect information about workers by keeping them under some form of observation, normally with a view to checking their performance or conduct.

The Code of Practice applies to systematic rather than occasional monitoring. Examples which fall within the Code of Practice are as follows:
- routinely recording the activities of employees by CCTV cameras;
- randomly opening up individual employees' emails or listening to their voicemails to look for evidence of malpractice;
- routinely examining logs of websites to check that individual employees are not downloading pornography.

Examples given of matters falling outside the Code of Practice include keeping records of customer transactions, as the data in this case is not processed primarily to keep a watch on employees' performance or conduct.

The Code of Practice contains two key principles, the concept of an 'impact assessment' and the need for a policy on monitoring.

Whilst Part 3 of the Code of Practice on monitoring only expressly applies to systematic monitoring, any monitoring, even occasional, may benefit from a basic 'impact assessment' to ensure it complies with the third data protection principle (DPA 1998, Sch 1).

Impact assessments

Impact assessments are based on the **data protection principles** which have been discussed above, and entail the employer having to do the following:

- identify clearly the **purposes** behind the monitoring and the benefits it is likely to deliver;
- identify any likely **adverse impact** of the monitoring arrangement;
- consider **alternatives** to monitoring and different ways in which it might be carried out;
- take into account the **obligations** that arise from the monitoring; and
- judge whether the monitoring is **justified** in the circumstances.

We look at each of these in turn below. Impact assessments do not necessarily have to be formal processes or documents and the Information Commissioner even suggests that, where appropriate, the process can be a quick mental one.

Impact assessments are more easily evidenced in writing and the more complex the issues, the more likely there is a need for a written impact assessment. From a practical perspective, employers may wish to keep some form of written record should it be necessary to justify their actions subsequently.

CLEAR PURPOSES

To be able to weigh up the advantages to the employer against any adverse impact on the employee or others, the employer needs to know why it is conducting the monitoring and what benefits it hopes to deliver.

Example: A company carries out covert CCTV monitoring of its employees for the purposes of preventing thefts of stock from a warehouse. In carrying out monitoring, the CCTV footage shows that employees are taking longer-than-allowed tea breaks. The Code of Practice would not justify the use of the CCTV footage for disciplinary actions in relation to excessive tea breaks. Practically speaking, if CCTV footage is used in these circumstances, the evidence is likely to be admissible in any subsequent litigation (see the section 'Admissibility of evidence obtained through monitoring' below), but it may affect whether any subsequent dismissal is fair under UK employment legislation.

ADVERSE IMPACT

Considering the likely adverse impact of monitoring requires considering the intrusion into private lives which will occur as a result of monitoring; the extent to which employees should be aware of monitoring to allow them to take it into account in their behaviour; limiting involvement in monitoring to those specific employees who 'need to know'; the impact on the trust and confidence between employer and employee; the impact on legitimate interests such as trade union discussions; and the extent to which monitoring would be demeaning. Considering the likely adverse impact of monitoring also requires considering the adverse effect of monitoring on those who are not necessarily the subject of that monitoring, for example the impact on members of the general public of CCTV cameras, even where CCTV cameras do not have those individuals as their focus.

ALTERNATIVES

Employers need to ask whether there is a less intrusive way of carrying out monitoring which would serve the same purpose, for example effective training and clearer communication of various policies (such as internet use). Also, if the monitoring is to combat misuse of systems, could monitoring be limited to employees about whom complaints have been received?

CONSIDERATION OF LEGAL OBLIGATIONS

Employers must consider the various legal obligations arising from monitoring, for example the extent to which employees should be informed and/or their consent sought regarding the monitoring; and employers' obligations both in processing the information and keeping it securely.

JUDGING WHETHER THE MONITORING IS JUSTIFIED

The final decision on whether to monitor amounts to a cost/benefit analysis, taking into account the benefits of monitoring, the 'cost' to employees in terms of privacy and whether there are alternative methods of achieving the purpose of monitoring, with particular emphasis on the principle that there should be no more intrusion than is absolutely necessary.

In carrying out the impact assessment, the Code of Practice provides a set of 'core principles':

- It will usually be intrusive to monitor your workers.
- Workers have legitimate expectations that they can keep their personal lives private and that they are also entitled to a degree of privacy in the work environment.
- If employers wish to monitor workers, they should be clear about the purpose and be satisfied that the particular monitoring arrangement is justified by real benefits that will be delivered.
- Workers should be aware of the nature, extent and reasons for any monitoring, unless (exceptionally) covert monitoring is justified.
- In any event, workers' awareness will influence their expectations.

Monitoring policies

The second key principle in the Code of Practice is the need for employers to have clear policies on the monitoring of electronic communications.

The Code of Practice only refers expressly to the need for employers to have policies on monitoring of electronic communications. Nevertheless, where there is systematic monitoring of a different nature, for example, personal searches, there is no reason why the same principle should not apply.

The Code of Practice requires the following:
- the policy should set out clearly the circumstances in which employees may or may not use telephone, email and internet systems. General bans on transmission of 'offensive material' are unlikely to be sufficiently clear; specific examples should be given;
- there should be some alternative ways available for employees to communicate confidentially, for example with a company doctor;
- where there is monitoring, the purposes for which communications are monitored should be explicit; and
- policies should explain how they will be enforced and the penalties which exist for breach of the policy.

What should email and internet policies contain?

Detailed written policies are a good opportunity for a business to set out not only the general business aims underlying the policy, but also the parameters of behaviour expected of employees in the course of their use of the systems/communications. This may assist in reducing the need to monitor. By setting the parameters, the employer can seek to prevent practical problems that can arise and can have a reference point should disciplinary action need to be taken against an employee.

An example of a basic email/internet policy is contained in Appendix G. The following should be considered for inclusion:

Purposes of monitoring

GENERAL BUSINESS AIMS

An employer can reinforce the primary reasons for the use of its IT system – furtherance of its business, conducting business in a professional manner and managing relationships with staff and clients.

FORMATION OF CONTRACTUAL COMMITMENTS

Employers can emphasise that emails can form the basis of an enforceable contract in the same way as an oral promise, a single line letter or a hundred page document.

Readers may be aware of the well-publicised embarrassments about emails which have been circulated throughout the world by employees. Problems arise because people are casual in emails in a way that they would not be in a formal letter. It should also be recognised that within minutes emails can be on the screens of potentially millions of users. A written policy is the most appropriate way for employers to remind their staff of this so as to establish patterns of behaviour which are less likely to result in adverse publicity.

CONSEQUENCES

In addition to issues surrounding content and distribution, employers can also use the policy to raise awareness amongst staff about viruses and systems integrity generally and thereby encourage the management of risk.

Policies do not need to be drafted as lists of prohibited behaviour, which may be detrimental to morale. Employers are increasingly aware that employees expect a degree of latitude in the workplace and a policy can send out a positive message to support this as well as protecting the business when it comes to enforcement.

Reasons for monitoring that an employer may wish to include in a purpose statement contained in a policy are:
- to ensure that the risk of viruses corrupting the system is minimised;
- to comply with any regulatory requirements concerning transactions;
- to prevent copyright infringement/defamation;
- to protect confidential information (although this might be achievable by limited monitoring only of those who have access to trade secrets);
- to ensure that there is no personal use or excessive personal use of the employer's systems; and
- to ensure that there is no harassment/ discrimination.

When using monitoring as a means of enforcement it is important that the reasons given are genuine, and do apply to the employer's business, as the Code of Practice makes clear that the reason for and necessity of monitoring will be subject to scrutiny. Employers should also avoid the temptation to list all the reasons for monitoring on the basis that any of them may apply at some time in the future. The reasons should be linked to the type and level of monitoring undertaken to give a rational and objective basis for justifying an employer's monitoring activities.

Extent of monitoring

In addition to the reasons for monitoring, it is important for the employer to say what sort of monitoring it plans to do. If the intention is to carry out continuous monitoring, then the policy should refer to this and explain the rationale – this will be relevant if the employer faces a tribunal claim or proceedings under the DPA 1998 and has to justify its actions.

If, on the other hand, the employer's practice will be to use technology for spot-checks as and when a problem arises, for example when a computer server gets clogged by large attachments to emails, then the employer should say so.

Enforcement of the policy

As reiterated by the Information Commissioner in the Code of Practice, the policy should set out the consequences for employees of misuse of the employer's systems and/or breach of the policy. Best practice involves including a statement along the lines of:

Any breach of this policy may result in disciplinary action being taken against you. In serious cases, this may include dismissal without notice or pay in lieu of notice.

Although some staff might regard such a statement as being unfriendly, it is an essential element of employment policies that staff know the consequences of failure to adhere to their terms, particularly as personal data may ultimately be used in disciplinary hearings and consequently this will be a purpose for which the data has been processed.

Except in the case of covert monitoring (for more on which, see below) if an employer subsequently extends the range of monitoring or the purposes for which monitoring is carried out, the employer will need to communicate this change to its employees.

The policy should also address how an employer deals with retention of electronic documents. If employees delete emails regularly but these are retained on a central computer directory, which the employer may then access, employees should be told this. Moreover, in the supplementary guidance to the Code of Practice, the Information Commissioner recommends that all systems should make provision for a way for employees permanently to delete emails and documents from their system.

The Information Commissioner's suggestion of provision for permanent deletion of emails may not be practical for business emails. An employer who allows employees the ability permanently to delete emails would then be relying upon employees to choose the correct emails to delete, something which may not be realistic. The converse situation may also apply, namely that it may be difficult for employers to sort between business-related and personal emails when deciding what emails on a computer should be the subject of a permanent back-up. These issues are discussed in further detail in the employment records chapter.

Communication of the policy

Effective communication of the contents of any policy is essential, not only under the DPA 1998, but also under the HRA 1998 and the Lawful Business Practice Regulations. There are alternative views (see Chapter 1 for a detailed discussion of consent) as

to whether employees should expressly agree to the contents of any policy and to any monitoring that is conducted under it. Various alternatives are:

- acknowledging the policy in employees' contracts of employment and providing for the express agreement of employees to the monitoring and recording of their activities by signature of those contracts;
- having the employees sign separate acknowledgments of the contents of the policy and their agreement to monitoring and recording;
- giving employees a copy of the policy or handbook and asking them to acknowledge they have received it; or
- giving employees notice of the policy or handbook in which the policy is contained without requiring any express acknowledgment or consent.

If either of the first two alternatives is to be used, employers could use wording along the following lines:

By signing these terms you acknowledge and agree that the Company may monitor and record both the volume and content of your email traffic and internet usage for the purposes of ensuring compliance with the Company's policy on the use of technology.

A policy included in a company handbook is not, without more, the ideal method of communication. It is a good idea to have some additional method of drawing employees' attention to it. Further, it is recommended that if the policy is to be enforced regular reminders are sent to staff directing them to the policy. Such reminders could be sent on a global email or included in a staff newsletter or bulletin and as a rule of thumb should be sent every three months.

Other kinds of monitoring considered in the Code of Practice

As well as emphasising the need for a policy in the context of electronic monitoring, the Code of

Practice also deals with other specific types of monitoring, including video and audio monitoring and 'in-vehicle monitoring'. The Code of Practice emphasises that video and audio monitoring should be targeted at areas at particular risk and confined to areas where expectations of privacy are low. It makes the point that continued video or audio monitoring of particular individuals is only likely to be justified in rare circumstances. As with general electronic monitoring, employees need to be given clear notification that monitoring is being carried out (except where covert monitoring is absolutely necessary, as to which see further below) and the purpose of such monitoring. Appropriate use of in-vehicle monitoring is similarly limited.

It is also important to be aware that third parties such as visitors or customers may inadvertently be caught by CCTV/audio monitoring and need to be made aware of its operation. The practical effect of this is that steps will need to be taken in terms of both positioning and signage of equipment such as video cameras. There is a separate code produced by the Information Commissioner on CCTV monitoring outside the employment relationship contained on the Information Commissioner's website, which is outside the scope of this work. That code is nevertheless very helpful when considering data protection issues arising out of CCTV monitoring.

Security of data obtained through monitoring

Security of data is covered generally in Part 2 of the Code of Practice on employment records and is dealt with in more detail in the employment records chapter. In the context of monitoring, the need for security is relevant in the areas set out below:

- Part 3 of the Code of Practice emphasises the need to provide monitoring data only to those who need to know, namely for the purposes of retrieving the information or for the purposes of assessing it. The more sensitive the data (particularly where there is covert monitoring involving sensitive personal data) the fewer the people who should have ultimate access to the information, for instance senior management

only. Particularly with regard to sensitive personal data and from the point of view of best practice, for all data retrieved by monitoring employers should consider using specially trained and vetted staff to carry out the monitoring, for example security staff who have been required to sign undertakings of confidentiality.

- The restriction of access to data should be backed up by audit trails which show which employees have had access to it.
- If equipment on which monitoring data is stored is taken away from the employer's premises, for example on laptop computers, this should be subject to rigorous control.

Covert monitoring

The Code of Practice states:

Covert monitoring should not normally be considered. It will be rare for covert monitoring of workers to be justified. It should therefore only be used in exceptional circumstances.

The Code of Practice also states that management should normally only authorise any covert monitoring on the basis that:

there are grounds for suspecting criminal activity or equivalent malpractice and notifying individuals about whether monitoring would prejudice its prevention or detection.

There is no explanation of 'equivalent malpractice', but there is the suggestion of malpractice of such seriousness that it would entitle an employer to notify the police, even if it does not actually do so.

Example: An employer suspects one of its employees of sexually harassing his secretary. The employer proposes to install a camera in the employee's office to obtain some proof. Can the employer do this?

Some issues to consider are:
- Has the employer carried out an impact assessment?
- What is the purpose of the proposed monitoring? Is it to catch the employee in the

act or is it to deter any future wrongdoing? Does the employer have reasonable grounds for suspecting the employee of sexual harassment?

- Will installing the camera achieve the objective of the employer? If it will, is there another less intrusive method of achieving the same result? Could the employer simply invite the employee's secretary to make a complaint which could then be investigated in accordance with the employer's usual practice?

- Who else is likely to be affected by the monitoring? Do others use the employee's office?

On balance, it is unlikely that covert monitoring could be justified in these circumstances, taking into account the intrusive nature of the proposed monitoring and balancing it against any benefit to the employer. An arguably more effective way of addressing the issue is to ask the employee's secretary to make a complaint. Covert monitoring is also unlikely to be justified in the circumstances as it is unlikely to achieve the employer's objective.

Monitoring of data and third parties

Third parties can be involved in two ways in the monitoring of employees. First, third parties can be used to carry out the monitoring on behalf of the employer, particularly in the context of covert monitoring, for example, private investigators. Secondly, third parties can hold data about individual employees which the employer may then decide to access. The following should be considered in this context:

- Private investigators
  Where a private investigator carries out an investigation on behalf of the employer, the employer will be a 'data controller' for the purposes of the DPA 1998, whilst the private investigator is likely to be a 'data processor', as he will not determine the manner in which or the purposes for the data is being processed. The consequence of this is that the employer, as data controller, will be responsible for the data being processed in a lawful manner and will be liable for the data processor's actions. This is discussed in further detail in

'Responsibilities of data controllers' in Chapter 1. Employers will therefore need to ensure that they have in place an adequate data processor agreement with a private investigator acting on their behalf setting out, for example, obligations of confidentiality and details of the data they have been instructed to obtain (and ensuring they keep within those parameters). Inadequate controls on third parties will render the employer ultimately liable for any infringement of the DPA 1998.

- Independent sources of information
  There are a variety of different organisations holding personal data on employees to which employers may have access, which will have consequences under the DPA 1998.

  For example, an employer may need to obtain information from the Criminal Records Bureau, because of the nature of the employee's job, although this is only permissible in very limited circumstances (further details are provided under 'Treatment of criminal record information' in the employment records chapter). Alternatively, employers may hold information about employees in a non-employment capacity, such as a bank whose employees are also its customers.

  The basic principles of the need for an impact assessment and a clear purpose for monitoring the data need to be applied. Information which has been monitored or obtained for one purpose should not be used for another. Consequently, information held by an employer which sells goods to some of its employees relating to credit rating should not be used as a way of vetting its employees for promotion.

Consent and privacy in the context of monitoring

It may be tempting for an employer carrying out monitoring to believe that the way to satisfy all of the requirements of the DPA 1998 and the Code of Practice is through obtaining employees' consent to the monitoring.

The issue of consent is discussed more fully in Chapter 1. As indicated there, the difficulty with consent is that the Information Commissioner has made it clear that he does not see consent as the primary way to satisfy the requirements in DPA 1998, Schs 2 and 3, rather consent should be used as a last resort.

A strategy of informing employees that monitoring is to take place rather than trying to obtain their consent may be possible, but employers need to be realistic about how general policy statements will be considered. For example, although a policy may refer to CCTV monitoring taking place anywhere in a building, employees may nevertheless have a legitimate expectation of privacy in toilets, something which is referred to expressly by the Information Commissioner. Equally, an organisation may have a culture whereby employees expect a certain degree of privacy, for example in a building which is not open plan, where employees each have their own office. In this case, such a culture may not be consistent with a right to search anywhere in the building.

The HRA 1998

The provisions of the HRA 1998 most relevant to employers carrying out monitoring will be the right to respect for private and family life (HRA 1998, Sch 1, art 8) and the right to a fair trial (HRA 1998, Sch 1, art 6) (which will be considered in the section 'Admissibility of evidence obtained through monitoring' below).

As a preliminary point, the applicability of the HRA 1998 will depend on the status of the employer. The HRA 1998 only applies directly to public authorities or 'quasi-public' bodies carrying out public functions, for example privatised utilities providing public services.

Consequently, employees of public authorities, for example civil servants, would be able to bring an action directly for a breach of the HRA 1998, including damages. For employees of private employers, however, there is no free-standing right to bring a claim for breach of the HRA 1998. However, it may be possible to bring a 'parasitic' claim

on the basis that courts and tribunals, as public bodies, are required to interpret the law in line with the HRA 1998. So, if there has been a breach of the HRA 1998 in obtaining evidence in a disciplinary proceeding, the fact that a right to privacy has been breached may render a dismissal unfair for the purposes of employment legislation and may result in an employment tribunal awarding damages for unfair dismissal.

The right to a private life

HRA 1998, Sch 1, art 8 states as follows:

> Everyone has the right to respect for his private and family life, his home and his correspondence.

> There shall be no interference by a public authority with the exercise of this right except such as is in accordance with the law and is necessary in a democratic society in the interests of national security, public safety or the economic well-being of the country, for the prevention of disorder or crime, for the prevention of health or morals, or for the protection of the rights and freedoms of others.

The concept of private life under the HRA 1998 extends to the workplace, for example to telephone calls made from business premises where there is an expectation of privacy. The key test is whether there is a reasonable expectation of privacy and this may be influenced by policy statements limiting expectations of privacy. However, as noted previously, universal statements about monitoring which are not specific or are not applied in practice are unlikely to be effective.

The right to privacy is not an absolute one. Employers will be able to justify interference with a right to privacy if it is in accordance with the law (which would not be the case if it amounted to a breach of the DPA 1998) and it is necessary for the protection of the rights and freedom of others, including the employer itself.

However, employers will still need to demonstrate that monitoring is proportionate and necessary to comply with the HRA 1998. As a result, those carrying out monitoring must have a clear idea of the purpose for which they are monitoring and must have considered whether there are alternatives to monitoring which would be as effective. In that sense, the HRA 1998 complements the DPA 1998 and compliance with the DPA 1998 is likely to achieve compliance with the HRA 1998.

RIPA 2000

RIPA 2000 created both civil and criminal liabilities relevant to monitoring. In short, RIPA 2000, s 1 provides that it is unlawful for a person, without lawful authority, intentionally to intercept a communication in the course of its transmission by way of a public or private telecommunication system. The Information Commissioner has referred expressly to RIPA 2000 in the Code of Practice.

RIPA 2000 does not apply to the processing of all data in the same way as the DPA 1998, rather there must be **interception** of some form of telecommunication, such as fax, email, or telephone. The definition of interception is fairly broad, including the accessing of emails which have been received by a recipient, stored in an 'incoming box' but not yet opened. However, emails which have already been opened and those emails which are in an 'outbox' as having already been sent would not, if accessed, fall within the meaning of interception within RIPA 2000.

Consequently, RIPA 2000 is likely to have most practical importance for the interception of unopened incoming emails or, for example, monitoring of access to sites whilst the employee is accessing those sites. A historic print-out of sites accessed is unlikely to amount to interception. It is permissible for an employer to intercept communications on its own telecommunication system where either the employee has consented, or where the purpose of the interception falls within one of six categories provided for under the Lawful Business Practice Regulations made pursuant to RIPA 2000. The purposes are:

- to create a record of transactions (for example evidence of an agreement between parties);
- to comply with regulatory or self-regulatory requirements (especially those employers in the financial services sector);
- to ensure that standards of service are maintained (for example in call centres);
- to prevent or detect crime;
- to investigate whether systems use is authorised (for example to comply with the employer's internet policy); and
- to secure the effective operation of a system (for example, to prevent viruses).

The various exemptions listed above are wider than the various criteria for monitoring under the DPA 1998. However, to rely on any of the exemptions, all reasonable efforts need to have been made to inform users of the telecommunication system of the interception. Practically speaking, employers are not expected to make all third parties aware of monitoring, rather only their own employees (although the DPA 1998 requires both). The employer would be expected, however, to take reasonable steps to inform third parties about the monitoring, for example by the use of a warning at the start of a telephone call to the effect that the call may be monitored, or by means of wording in an email disclaimer.

Also, interception under any of the above exceptions is only permissible if the interception is solely for the purposes of monitoring or keeping a record of communications relevant to the employer's business, when the telecommunication system is question is provided for **use wholly or partly in connection with that business**. The practical effects of this requirement are:
- if there are private telephone lines which have been expressly designated as such, there will be no lawful reason to intercept the communication; and
- if an employer adopts a policy of intercepting any and all communication on a random basis, regardless of whether that communication might relate to its business (for example private emails, where it allows private email use) it will breach RIPA 2000.

If there is any interception which is in breach of RIPA 2000, it will render any processing unlawful under the DPA 1998 (as the purpose will not be lawful under the first data protection principle).

Admissibility of evidence obtained through monitoring

The traditional approach to admissibility of evidence in the employment tribunals and in the higher courts governed by the Civil Procedure Rules is based on relevance. Prior to Civil Procedure Rules, there was no jurisdiction to exclude evidence in civil trials on the basis that it had been unlawfully obtained. Whilst the Civil Procedure Rules now provide discretion to exclude evidence which would otherwise be admissible (CPR 32.1) (for example, where a court decides that it will only hear evidence on a particular issue) the assumption remains that the courts do not have a general power to exclude admissible evidence. The employment tribunals are expressly not bound by any law relating to admissibility of evidence in the higher courts, but will be bound by the HRA 1998, including Sch 1, art 6, relating to the right to a fair trial.

Will evidence which has been obtained unlawfully, in breach of the DPA 1998, the HRA 1998 or any common law such as trespass or breach of confidence be inadmissible? There have been only a small number of cases considering the issue, but the current view is set out below.

- Courts will conduct a balancing exercise to weigh up the rights of the individual whose rights have been infringed against the ultimate relevance of the evidence.
- Evidence which is highly relevant is unlikely not to be admitted, on the grounds that HRA 1998, Sch 1, art 6 contains no requirements as to the admissibility of evidence and the European Court of Human Rights has left this issue to national courts; and that the fact that evidence has been gathered in breach of a convention right does not, of itself, make it inadmissible.

Note, however, the proposal for a new EU HR Directive on data protection (see Chapter 1) which, if adopted, would make evidence obtained in breach of the DPA 1998 inadmissible in courts or tribunals.

Monitoring in the workplace – summary of main issues
- Monitoring in the workplace can involve not only consideration of issues arising under the DPA 1998, but also under the HRA 1998 and RIPA 2000.
- The impact assessment is the key tool employers should use in determining whether monitoring is proportionate and necessary in any particular situation.
- Consent of employees is not usually required before an employer undertakes monitoring although employees will have to be informed when, how and why the monitoring is taking place.
- A detailed written policy in relation to use of email and the internet by employees is recommended both to ensure compliance with the DPA 1998 and to allow an employer to justify a dismissal for misuse of those systems under employment law more generally.
- Covert monitoring is almost never permissible.

Chapter 6

Issues arising on corporate transactions

Maya Cronly-Dillon

The purpose of this chapter is to review the data protection issues that employers should consider in the context of corporate transactions. This chapter looks specifically at share and business sales. Readers should note that the issues posed by a business sale may equally apply to an outsourcing. The term 'purchaser' in this chapter should therefore be read to include not only the purchaser of a business, but also a service provider to which staff may be transferred under the Transfer of Undertakings (Protection of Employment) Regulations 1981 (SI 1981/1794) ('TUPE') in an outsourcing situation.

This chapter will examine how the Data Protection Act 1998 impacts on the disclosure and due diligence process and the treatment of employment data by both vendor and purchaser during a transaction. It looks, in particular, at:

- ways in which a vendor may avoid the application of the DPA 1998 by anonymising data;
- information which the DPA 1998 requires a vendor and/or purchaser to give to employees before disclosing and/or using their personal data ('fair processing information');

- exemptions from the obligation to provide fair processing information;
- other conditions to be satisfied in order for the 'processing' of personal data to be fair (namely, via either the 'legitimate business interest' or the 'consent' route); and
- the risks of non-compliance.

Overview

There are a number of stages during a commercial transaction where an employer/vendor may need to disclose information, with varying degrees of detail, about its workforce to a third party. Information may need to be provided:

- at the bidding stage;
- after an initial offer has been accepted;
- after exchange of contracts; and
- on completion.

Where 'personal data' may be disclosed as part of this process, the DPA 1998 may require a vendor (or the purchaser who is to review the information) to inform employees about this process or even to obtain individual consent to discuss and use the information in a particular way. For more details on what constitutes personal data, see Chapter 1.

The part of the Employment Practices Data Protection Code of Practice (the 'Code of Practice') on employment records, Part 2, at section 13, entitled 'Mergers and Acquisitions' sets out some guidance on how to approach disclosure of employee information in a transactional context. This guidance is not legally binding, but represents the Information Commissioner's recommendations as to how to achieve compliance with the DPA 1998. The current Information Commissioner has indicated that he is going to revisit this Part of the Code of Practice. What follows is based on the version of Part 2 in existence at the date of this Report.

The Code of Practice sets out six practical benchmarks for the disclosure of employee data in mergers and acquisitions and these are reproduced in Appendix H.

In practice, parties to some transactions may struggle to comply with all the principles of the DPA 1998

without jeopardising commercial confidentiality, particularly where a proposed transaction is price-sensitive. In these situations, vendors and purchasers often need to take a pragmatic and informed approach to minimising and/or managing the risks of non-compliance. This chapter gives guidance on the issues to be considered in carrying out this delicate balancing act.

Anonymising data for due diligence purposes

During the due diligence and disclosure stages of a transaction, the data protection issues will be similar regardless of whether the deal involves the transfer of assets or of shares. A purchaser may want to review information about:

- officers;
- employees;
- former employees and pensioners;
- directors; and/or
- consultants and agency workers.

Generic, anonymous information about the workforce from which individuals cannot be identified (that is, data which is not 'personal') falls outside the DPA 1998 so the disclosure of this information by employers should not pose a problem. However, information from which actual individuals can be identified is 'personal data' and disclosing or transferring that data to a prospective purchaser will amount to **processing** that data and therefore falls within the scope of the DPA 1998. (For more detail on the general principles which apply to the fair processing of personal data see Chapter 1.)

In creating a data room for prospective bidders in the early stages of a transaction, a vendor may not need to disclose information relating to specific employees. A vendor may need merely to provide prospective purchasers with an overview of the employment issues (such as a breakdown of how many employees of a particular kind are employed in a particular area or field, and their average rates of pay). One approach to anonymising personal information is to replace each employee's name with a number. Where employees' names are replaced with numbers, vendors should maintain a key of the names and numbers to ensure the data can be verified post-acquisition. The Code of Practice goes further and suggests that, in some cases, individual job titles should also be omitted as this may lead to the identification of an individual (for example, where even without the name it is obvious that the information relates to a particular senior manager). Moreover, the Code of Practice notes that even if the removal of names from the data provided will not prevent identification by certain recipients of the individuals to whom that information relates, at the very least it may go some way towards protecting privacy generally.

Completely anonymous information may not always be acceptable to a potential purchaser, even at an early stage. For example, if a target company is only a viable investment if there are possible areas in which to rationalise the workforce, a purchaser may need some indication of how many managers there are in a particular area, or what employees' job functions are so that it can consider the prospects of conducting such an exercise.

Certainly, once a bid is accepted and a transaction progresses, a purchaser will often ask for more detailed information relating to specific individuals. In certain cases, especially where the value of the business may depend heavily upon the skills of certain employees, a purchaser will be justified in asking to see specific information relating to them. The anonymisation requirement can also be difficult to achieve with directors or senior executives, where it is often important to relate the information in the data room to a particular individual, for example, to determine what restrictive covenants apply to a key executive, whether he can be placed on garden leave or how long his notice period is. In practice, it may be easier to conform to the data protection principles and inform individuals in senior management that their personal data will be disclosed if, unlike the rest of the workforce, they are aware of the transaction and the same risks to confidentiality do not apply.

The box following sets out a checklist of preliminary questions a vendor should consider in compiling a data room.

Checklist of preliminary questions: preparing a data room

1. Vendors and purchasers need to consider what information a purchaser really needs and when.
2. Look carefully (and critically) at the categories or type of data which a purchaser is asking for. This will usually be indicated by a formal information request.
3. Some information may not be necessary for a purchaser at an early due diligence stage, when there are a number of prospective bidders, but it may become important at a later stage.
4. Consider the possibility of anonymising data so that it is not personal data. Consider if identification of individuals could arise even from the anonymised data. Is it practicable to avoid this happening? If not, could the individual be prejudiced by being identified in connection with the information provided?
5. Could the request, if complied with, lead to the disclosure of personal or sensitive personal data or even data relating to non-employees (such as spouses, partners and children)? If the personal data is sensitive personal data, explicit consent to the disclosure would ordinarily need to be sought.
6. Purchasers must accept there may be concerns about disclosing personal data to them, particularly if it is sensitive personal data (such as sickness records). If, as sometimes happens, a purchaser objects to the anonymisation of data, interpreting it as an attempt to conceal material information, it may be worth reminding the purchaser that were it to receive personal data in a data room, it would become a data controller in respect of that personal data. This means it would itself be under an obligation to inform employees of the use it is making of their personal data in the sale process (see Chapter 1 for more detail on the obligations of data controllers).
7. Ensure that data room rules (whether physical or online/virtual) address the need for the security of personal data.
8. Individual employees could monitor how their personal data is being presented and check-up on a vendor's compliance by way of a subject access request. If personal data is held in a

relevant filing system in the data room, an individual might ask to see what information is being disclosed about him.

Fair processing information and conditions

What steps need to be taken in order to disclose and/or use personal data in a data room?

The data protection principle most relevant to any transactional disclosure exercise is that any personal data must be processed 'fairly and lawfully' (the first principle). The DPA 1998 requires **both** the vendor who discloses information **and** the purchaser to whom personal data is disclosed to:

- inform employees of the disclosure of their personal data and of the parties who will be the recipients of that information; and
- ensure that one of the 'fair processing' conditions set out in DPA 1998, Sch 2 (or, in the case of sensitive personal data, DPA 1998, Sch 3) (see Chapter 1) is satisfied.

A vendor can notify employees of these matters on its own behalf and on behalf of the purchaser if need be.

Fair processing information

Fair processing information must include:

- the identity of the data controller. In the context of a due diligence exercise, the term 'data controller' will encompass both the employer/ vendor who provides information to the data room and the prospective purchaser who will be using the information provided as part of its assessment of the business;
- the purposes for which the data will be processed; and
- any other information that is necessary to enable the particular processing to be fair.

In practice, the Information Commissioner has acknowledged in Part 2, Section 13 of the Code of Practice that in the context of a transaction, vendors

and purchasers may, for reasons of commercial confidentiality, find it very difficult to provide employees with the fair processing information which the DPA 1998 requires before exchange of contracts or, in some cases, before the transaction completes. Advising employees when they join an organisation that their personal data may, if their employer is involved in a commercial transaction, need to be disclosed for the purposes of due diligence may go some way towards fulfilling the fair processing information obligations at a later date.

On completion of a share sale, there will be no change in the identity of the employer/data controller and no additional fair processing information need be given after completion, except where the new owner of the shares proposes to use the data for a new purpose.

Fair processing issues may arise if employees feel it is important that they have given their data to their employer as a member of a particular group of companies. This could happen in respect of information given in relation to retirement benefits, or long-term disability benefits which arise under a group scheme. The transfer of the target to a new group may, in the circumstances, require the target to update the fair processing information to report on the change of group.

On a business sale or where employees are transferred in the context of an outsourcing, there will be a transfer of employee records containing personal data from the vendor to the purchaser. As both the disclosure and receipt of personal data in these circumstances will amount to processing, both parties will be under a duty to inform the employees that their personal data is now being held by a new employer.

In practice, it is sufficient for one of the parties to fulfil this obligation and, because the vendor will no longer be the data controller of that data, it is common for the purchaser to notify its new employees on behalf of both parties. If a vendor relies on the purchaser to contact its former employees on its behalf, it should obtain assurances from the purchaser (usually documented in the sale agreement) that this will be done. Vendors often seek to agree with the purchaser the text of the fair processing notice to ensure that it is consistent with the general message being publicised by the vendor regarding the sale.

Examples of fair processing information notices for use during and on completion of a transaction appear at Appendix I.

Exemptions from the obligation to provide fair processing information

Corporate finance exemption

Where notifying employees about the processing of their personal data could affect the price of a company's shares or other financial instruments, or could prejudice an important economic or financial interest of the UK, the parties to a transaction may need to consider if they can rely on the 'corporate finance exemption' provisions contained in the DPA 1998, Sch 7, para 6 and the Data Protection (Corporate Finance Exemption) Order 2000 (SI 2000/184).

There have been no reported cases to date on the scope of this exemption and it is difficult to gauge just how wide its application might be.

Business transfers and TUPE

In business transfers (or outsourcing transactions) TUPE requires a purchaser/transferee to inform a vendor/transferor about its future plans for the transferring workforce, long enough before a transfer to allow the vendor/transferor to fulfil its obligation to conduct an information and consultation exercise with representatives of the workforce about those plans.

The Code of Practice suggests that where there is a legal obligation to disclose personal data, there is an exemption from some of the provisions of the DPA 1998. It states:

The employer is relieved of the obligation to inform workers of the disclosure if this would

be inconsistent with the disclosure, perhaps because it would breach commercial confidentiality.

The logic behind this assertion is questionable.

The reason for non-disclosure of fair processing information to the workforce would, in the example given by the Code of Practice, be due to commercial confidentiality. In fact, the only provisions allowing for non-disclosure of fair processing information due to reasons of commercial confidentiality are contained in the corporate finance exemption outlined above.

TUPE implicitly requires the vendor to disclose employee information to the purchaser so that the purchaser, in turn, can inform the vendor of the employment related measures it proposes to take. This information is disclosed to the workforce as part of the statutory information and consultation exercise which the vendor or transferor needs to undertake before the transfer. That exercise also requires the vendor, among other things, to inform the workforce of the transfer. Therefore commercial confidentiality may not be a sufficient reason to justify failure to notify employees that their personal data is to be given to a purchaser for this purpose.

It might be possible for the purchaser to form a preliminary view of its plans on the basis of generic employee information provided in a data room (especially if there are standard terms and conditions of employment and the purchaser is not proposing any radical measures). Then, time permitting, the vendor could wait until the workforce knows of the transaction before disclosing personal data which will then be used by the purchaser to finalise its plans. At this stage, there should be no confidentiality issue preventing the vendor from notifying employees about the disclosure of their personal data to the purchaser for the consultation process.

The DPA 1998, Sch 2, para 3 provides that processing is lawful if it is necessary for compliance with any legal obligation to which the data subject is subject other than an obligation imposed by contract. However, this deals with fair processing conditions, not fair processing information.

It is difficult to see why TUPE might provide an exemption from the obligation to notify employees whose personal data is disclosed for ordinary due diligence purposes where no such exemption is available in the context of a share sale. The DPA 1998 issues surrounding data rooms and due diligence are largely the same where a transaction is a business transfer or a share sale. In short, the guidance issued by the Code of Practice on this point needs to be approached with some caution.

Fair processing conditions: the 'legitimate business interests' or 'consent' route

In addition to providing the fair processing information, data controllers (vendors or purchasers) must also ensure that the way in which they use employees' personal data (that is, its 'processing') falls within, or can be justified under, one of the fair processing conditions in the DPA 1998, Sch 2 (see Chapter 1).

In essence, a vendor will either need to show that disclosure and/or use of the data is necessary for one of a number of specified purposes or that employee consent has been obtained.

The most commonly relied upon condition used by a vendor and prospective purchaser to justify disclosure and/or receipt of personal data for due diligence purposes and then the ultimate transfer of personal data (in the context of a business sale) to the purchaser is on the basis that it is within their legitimate business interests to do so (the 'legitimate interest condition').

Legitimate business interests

One of the conditions in DPA 1998, Sch 2 which will allow a vendor to disclose personal data without seeking consent is that:

> the processing is necessary for the purposes of a legitimate interest pursued by the data controller or by the third party or parties to whom the data [is] disclosed, except where the processing is unwarranted in any particular

case by reason of prejudice to the rights and freedoms or legitimate interests of the data subject.

There is a balancing act to be achieved. Some thought still needs to be given to whether or not it might be prejudicial to the interests of the employees to have their data disclosed in these circumstances. If, for example, a purchaser was to use the information it had received (such as details of past disciplinary offences) to put pressure on a vendor to dismiss or carry out redundancies of certain individuals before completion as a result of the disclosure of personal data, then arguably those employees could complain that the disclosure of information about them to the purchaser which could have led to their dismissal was prejudicial to their interests.

Vendors and purchasers often rely on the legitimate business interest condition (as obtaining employee consent pre-completion may be impracticable) on the grounds that the transfer of data in connection with a sale or acquisition of an asset is in the vendor's or purchaser's legitimate interests and would not prejudice the rights or freedoms or the legitimate interests of the data subject. In an asset sale, the obligation on the purchaser to preserve the employees' old terms and conditions of employment once their employment transfers, and to provide information to a vendor in order to facilitate consultation with the workforce before completion, would probably make the transfer of personal data justifiable under the legitimate interest condition, but in the later stages of the transaction.

This is usually fine so far as personal data is concerned, but will not be acceptable in the case of sensitive personal data (see discussion of the fair processing conditions for sensitive personal data in Chapter 1). To justify the disclosure and use of sensitive personal data under current arrangements is almost impossible in the absence of explicit consent.

Consent

The DPA 1998 does not define consent although EC Directive 95/46/EC on the protection of individuals with regard to the processing of personal data and free movement of such data defines a data subject's consent as:

> any freely given specific and informed indication of his wishes by which the data subject signifies his agreement to personal data relating to him being processed.

The Information Commissioner has made it clear that obtaining consent is not easy to achieve. The quality of the consent must also be assessed. Where the data subject feels he has no option but to consent (which may be the case where someone is threatened with dismissal or the loss of promotion prospects) it may be that consent is not freely given. Consent will also need to be informed. This means the employee must know and have understood what he is agreeing to.

Consent to the processing of sensitive personal data (such as sickness records or information about an employee's sexuality) is even more stringent in that it needs to be explicit – this means it must relate to the very specific circumstances of the disclosure being contemplated. General consents to processing sensitive personal data given at the beginning of an employment relationship will not suffice.

Even where employees are unlikely to object to the transfer of their personal data to prospective purchasers, if the workforce is large, obtaining the appropriate consents from every individual might be impractical and/or may be precluded for reasons of commercial confidentiality. A vendor may need to consider other options. The general difficulties of the consent route are discussed in more detail in Chapter 1.

The Government has promised to address this difficulty in the TUPE context in its upcoming TUPE reform. The intention is to impose a legal obligation on a vendor to supply certain employee information to a purchaser. This would mean that a fair processing condition from both Schs 2 and 3 would be satisfied, removing one obstacle to the transfer of employee data in a transactional context.

To comply or not to comply? Assessing the risks

Given the pressures on a purchaser to ascertain the scope of potential liabilities and obligations in relation to the workforce of a target organisation, often before exchange of contracts, vendors will frequently be required to make judgements about the extent to which personal data should be disclosed, even if such disclosure is in technical breach of the DPA 1998. They will need to consider to what extent any failure to comply with the data protection principles in disclosing personal data may prejudice the employees' rights or interests (aside from the breach of the DPA 1998) and the risks of repercussions or action being taken against them.

Breach of the data protection principles is not a criminal offence. However, the Information Commissioner has the power to issue an enforcement notice (irrespective of whether a complaint has been made by an aggrieved employee) requiring the employer to comply with the relevant principle or cease to offend within a specified period. Failure to comply with such a notice is a criminal offence.

A vendor or purchaser may also face civil proceedings where an employee has suffered damage, or damage and distress (but not distress alone), as a result of the data controller's failure to comply with the principles. More detail on enforcement generally can be found in Chapter 1.

Certain acts of non-compliance may carry greater risks than others. In particular, it will be recalled that enforcement is a discretionary remedy. The Information Commissioner has acknowledged that in certain circumstances it can be difficult to satisfy the requirements of the legislation. In such circumstances, in considering whether to exercise discretion to enforce, the Information Commissioner would look carefully at the nature of the processing, taking into account any damage and distress caused to the data subject as a result of that processing. The fact that the purchaser had signed a confidentiality agreement in respect of the data disclosed so that the information went no further would be relevant here, as would the fact that the purchaser, when it becomes the employer, should not deal with the data in any different way than the vendor did.

Some other factors to consider are set out below:

- if the breach of a fair processing principle (such as disclosing personal details without employees' knowledge) is a 'one off', then is the organisation prepared to risk being issued with an enforcement notice? Once a vendor has sold the business and the due diligence exercise is completed then it may not need to commit any further breaches;

- failure by an organisation which has become the employer of staff by way of a TUPE transfer and which receives personnel records from the previous employer to notify those employees that it is the new data controller will be an on-going breach of the fair processing principle. Continued use of the data will make it impossible to view the failing as a one-off breach;

- if an employee is personally prejudiced as a result of the vendor or purchaser's breach of the fair processing principles and is caused damage, the risk of employees taking civil action against the offending party should be considered in addition to the risk of an enforcement or information notice from the Information Commissioner;

- a failure to comply with the requirement to obtain explicit consent to the disclosure and use of sensitive personal data (such as sickness records, information about a person's religion or sexuality or race and so on) is likely to be viewed more seriously and therefore prejudice in the form of damage and distress to the individual will be easier to show;

- if it comes to light that an organisation has flagrantly and insensitively flouted the data protection principles, even a one-off breach could cause a degree of reputational damage;

- is there scope for a breach to be 'remedied' at a later date, for example, where employees have not been given the fair processing information but are told once the deal is completed that the purchaser has reviewed and now holds their personal data?

- a vendor can take steps to limit any potential damage caused by breach of a fair processing principle by insisting upon stringent confidentiality undertakings and assurances by the purchaser, or by providing in the sale agreement that the purchaser must provide fair processing information post-completion. (See Appendix J for some sample wording for a confidentiality undertaking);

- vendors should also check whether employees have ever been warned in the past that their personal data might be disclosed to a prospective purchaser and to what extent this warning might satisfy the fair processing information requirements in relation to the transaction being considered.

Transfers of data outside the European Economic Area (EEA) in breach of the eighth principle are likely to be judged severely by the Information Commissioner as the exporting of data to a non-adequate territory will effectively mean that the data subjects will lose their protections under the DPA 1998. More detail on this topic can be found in the next chapter.

Data protection in corporate transactions – summary of main issues

- In any corporate transaction both the vendor and purchaser should think carefully about the level of employee data it is necessary to disclose at each stage of the transaction.
- At the due diligence stage of a transaction it will often be appropriate to disclose employee data only in anonymised form.
- If it becomes necessary to disclose employee personal data as part of the transaction, consideration has to be given to compliance with both the requirement to give employees fair processing information and the requirement to satisfy one of the fair processing conditions.
- Often in a corporate transaction, full compliance with the DPA 1998 will not be desirable or even possible from a commercial perspective. In those situations, organisations have to give careful consideration to the risks of non-compliance.

Chapter 7

Transfers of data overseas

Heather Rowe

This chapter explores data protection issues relating to transfers of data outside the European Economic Area (EEA) (that is, the European Union, Iceland, Norway and Liechtenstein).

Cross-border transfers from the UK

The eighth data protection principle in the Data Protection Act 1998 ('the DPA 1998') reflects Arts 25 and 26 of the EC directive on the protection of individuals with regard to the processing of personal data and the free movement of such data (Directive 95/46/EC) ('the Directive'). Breach of this principle is not immediately a criminal offence, but is subject to the procedure for enforcing data protection principles, including enforcement notices (see 'Enforcement', Chapter 1 for further detail).

The eighth data protection principle says:

> Personal data shall not be transferred to a country or territory outside the European

Economic Area unless that country or territory ensures an adequate level of protection for the rights and freedoms of data subjects in relation to the processing of personal data.

Further interpretation of adequacy is contained in DPA 1998, Sch 1:

An adequate level of protection is one which is adequate in all the circumstances of the case, having regard in particular to:
(a) the nature of the personal data;
(b) the country or territory of origin of the information contained in the data;
(c) the country or territory of final destination of that information;
(d) the purposes for which and period during which the data are intended to be processed;
(e) the law in force in the country or territory in question;
(f) the international obligations of that country or territory;
(g) any relevant codes of conduct or other rules which are enforceable in that country or territory (whether generally or by arrangement in particular cases); and
(h) any security measures taken in respect of the data in that country or territory.

If a UK data controller believes, after careful assessment, that the level of protection **is** adequate in a particular country, the Information Commissioner has indicated that the data controller can proceed without consulting the Information Commissioner. However, before making an assessment, a look is recommended at the Information Commissioner's paper 'The Eighth Data Protection Principle and Transborder Dataflows' (which is available at www.information commissioner.gov.uk/cms/documentsuploads/ transborder%20dataflows.pdf). This explains how to go about an adequacy assessment. Theoretically it is possible that there could be a subsequent challenge to the adequacy view and the Information Commissioner could commence enforcement proceedings. An exporter of data must 'be able to defend its actions should it be called on to do so subsequently'.

DPA 1998, Sch 4 sets out circumstances where, even if the transferee country provides *inadequate* protection and the data exporter has not been able to establish adequacy in some way, transfers can take place. **One** of a number of conditions needs to be met. The most likely to apply in an employment context are that:

(a) the data subject has given his *consent* to the transfer;
(b) transfer is necessary for the:
   (i) *performance of a contract between the data subject and the data controller [that is the employment contract];* or
   (ii) *taking* of *steps* at the request of the data subject *with a view to his entering into a contract* with the data controller [for example, sending a job applicant's details overseas where the decision to employ is taken there];
(c) transfer is *necessary for the purpose of:*
   (i) or in connection with, any *legal proceedings* (including prospective legal proceedings);
   (ii) *obtaining legal advice,* or
   (iii) of *establishing, exercising or defending legal rights;*
(d) transfer is necessary in order *to protect the data subject's vital interests* [this is very narrow – for example, an employee is badly hurt overseas and certain medical data is needed to help him];
(e) transfer is made *on terms [such as a contract] approved* by the Commissioner as ensuring adequate safeguards for data subjects' rights and freedoms;
(f) transfer has been authorised by the Commissioner as being made *in such a manner as to ensure adequate safeguards for the rights and freedoms of data subjects.*

Where a UK company decides, say, to send all its HR data to be hosted on a parent company's systems in the US, in order to cut costs and make the processing of employee data more efficient, it must consider which condition to rely on (if adequacy has not been established by another means, such as Model Contracts, see further below). One might argue that such a transfer is necessary for the performance of a contract between the data subject and the data controller (namely the employment contract), because that is how the group of companies processes data necessary for the employment contract, such as payment of expenses and salary.

However, the Information Commissioner has published a paper (available from www.information commissioner.gov.uk), entitled 'International Transfers of Personal Data' which looks at what is 'necessary for the performance of a contract':

In this context, contracts are not restricted to goods and services. These provisions will, for example, be relevant in the case of employment contracts. The Information Commissioner takes the view that determination of whether a transfer is 'necessary' for the performance of a contract depends on the nature of the goods, services etc provided under the contract rather than the business structure of the data controller. A transfer is not 'necessary' if the only reason it is needed is because of the way a data controller has chosen to structure its business.

So, where a corporate group reorganises its global HR processing into a country outside the EEA, if that data was either formerly processed satisfactorily in the EEA Member States, or could be processed in the EEA, the employer will not be able to rely on this condition.

In the above example, the only conditions which may be relied on are consent or contractual terms.

The DPA 1998 does not define consent, but the Directive says it must be 'freely given, specific and informed'. (See Chapter 1 for more detail on this issue.)

One of the Information Commissioner's papers on transfers says:

Consent must be freely given. It can be made a condition for the provision of a non-essential service but consent is unlikely to be valid if the data subject has no real choice but to give his/her consent. For example, if an existing

employee is required to agree to the international transfer of personal data any consent given is unlikely to be valid if the penalty for not agreeing is dismissal. Consent must also be specific and informed. The data subject must know and have understood what he/she is agreeing to. The reasons for the transfer and as far as possible the countries involved should be specified. If the data controller is aware of any particular risks involved in the transfer it should bring these to the data subject's attention.

This is important to bear in mind. Employees need to know what is happening to their data to satisfy the first data protection principle (see 'Data protection principles', Chapter 1). If seeking consent to transfer outside the EEA, the destination and any particular risks in the transfer must be explained.

The Information Commissioner has indicated that it may be easier to obtain a valid consent from prospective employees rather than, perhaps, from existing employees, although that observation was made in the context of 'explicit' consent to processing sensitive data.

Obtaining necessary informed consent should be part of the induction process for new employees. For existing employees, their consent could be obtained in a number of ways (again, see Chapter 1).

It **must** be borne in mind that, even if consent is not required under DPA 1998, Sch 4, Sch 2 and Sch 3 will still apply. If the data to be exported is sensitive personal data, explicit consent to the processing will very often be required under DPA 1998, Sch 3 (see 'DPA 1998, Sch 3 conditions' in Chapter 1).

The US 'safe harbor'

The EU recognised the importance of not disrupting dataflows to the US arising from enforcement of Arts 25 and 26 of the Directive. The EU and US governments have agreed a mechanism for transfers to the US, comprising a set of 'safe harbor' principles enabling ongoing transfers to US entities voluntarily agreeing to follow those principles (and publicly registering to that effect). The 'safe harbor' was approved on 31 May 2000 as a 'Community Finding' under Art 25(6), meaning that it provides adequacy of protection.

Some essentials of the safe harbor principles are:
(a) notice – about what information is collected on data subjects and how it is processed and used;
(b) choice – the ability for consumers to 'opt-out', especially from direct marketing;
(c) onward transfer – choice for individuals about how third parties use their data;
(d) security – reasonable measures to protect data from loss, misuse, and so on;
(e) data integrity – data to be kept accurate, current and complete;
(f) access – individuals to have reasonable access to information about them derived from non-public sources;
(g) enforcement – compliance mechanisms; recourse for individuals and so on.

The US Department of Commerce ('DOC') produces a list of adhering companies so that European exporters know where they can send data without seeking other safeguards. There are currently only around 400 subscribers since for US companies to change their processes to comply with the principles usually requires significant work.

Companies can subscribe to the principles for all their data or only for certain categories – for example human resources data, manually processed data or online data. This is interesting because it may be possible for a company to centralise its global HR processing on specific servers in the US, say, and for the US company involved to comply with the principles in respect of HR data on those ring-fenced servers, even if it is unable yet to do so for all its data. This will permit transfer of the HR data.

The safe harbor is not available currently to banks and certain other industries (such as telecommunications) which are not regulated by the US Federal Trade Commission (necessary to be a safe harbor participant). For them, alternatives like consent or Model Contracts are important.

Compliance is checked, initially, by certain privacy bodies approved by the Commission, but the ultimate legal sanction for non-compliance is enforcement action under The US Federal Trade Commission Act, which forbids misrepresentation and deceptive trade practices (such as publicly announcing adherence to the principles but breaching them).

For more information, visit the DOC website www.export.gov/safeharbor/sh_overview.html.

The use of contracts for the export of personal data

Under DPA 1998, Sch 4 Condition 9 (see above), the Information Commissioner can approve transfers 'made on terms [that is, contractual terms] which are of a kind approved by him'.

Papers from the Information Commissioner, referred to in 'Cross-border transfers from the UK' above, explore the provisions which should appear in such contracts and point out that certain industry bodies, like the International Chamber of Commerce, have produced model clauses which could be a base for such a contract. Since the Model Contracts were approved, the Information Commissioner encourages companies to use the Model Contracts, rather than bringing contracts to the Information Commissioner's office, case by case, for approval. However, the earlier advice has never been withdrawn, so it would still appear possible to create such a personalised contract (in compliance with the advice) if the Model Contracts are not palatable for some reason.

EU Model Contracts

Controller to controller transfers

The Commission approved a Model Contract for export between two 'data controllers' in June 2001 (for 'data controller', see Chapter 1), to be found on the Commission's website at: www.europa.eu.int/

com/internal_market/en/media/dataprot/news/clausesdecision.pdf.

In an inter-company transfer, what might constitute a transfer from data controller to data controller? This could arise if a European group company were to transfer employee data to its parent in the US, (for example, there is a shared database) and the European subsidiary is a data controller. The parent might **also** access that data for **its** purposes of taking global HR decisions, carrying out global assessments of employees or setting global criteria for future appointments (which would make it a data controller as well).

The Model Contract could be the adequacy solution for such exports. Some provisions, however, are potentially onerous. For example:

(a) EU data subjects are granted the right to enforce many clauses of the contract 'as third party beneficiaries';

(b) the data exporter agrees that if the transfer involves sensitive personal data, data subjects have been informed or will be informed before the transfer that this data could be transmitted to a third country not providing adequate protection. Thus, notifications to data subjects under the first data protection principle must spell this out;

(c) the clauses provide 'the Parties agree that Data Subjects who have suffered damage as a result of any violation of the provisions referred to in clause 3 [that is the third party beneficiary clause] are entitled to receive compensation from the party for the damage suffered';

(d) clause 6(2) provides 'the data exporter and the data importer agree that they will be *jointly and severally liable* for damage to the Data Subject resulting from any violation of the provisions referred to in clause 3. In the event of a violation of these obligations and/or conditions, the Data Subject can take action before a court against either of the Data Exporter or the Data Importer or both'.

Liability is **unlimited**. By clause 6 of the Model Contract, if one party is held liable for the other party's breach of the model, the second will agree

to indemnify the first – but that is clearly only as good as the defaulting party's balance sheet.

Liability risk is greater where transferring HR data to a third party data controller, because as a practical matter the data exporter must diligently vet the proposed contracting party, not only in relation to its security levels and technical capabilities, but also its financial standing and its ability to stand behind the undertakings in the Model Contract.

Controller to processor transfers

A Model Contract for export of data to a **data processor**, approved December 2001, is available from www.europa.eu.int/eur-lex/pri/en/oj/dat/2002/l_006/l_00620020110en00520062.pdf. It has some of the shortcomings of the controller-to-controller model.

The Information Commissioner has made it clear in the past that a *presumption* of adequacy *can* be made for most, if not all, transfers outside the EEA made by exporting controllers to overseas **processors**. This presumption arises because the exporting data controller necessarily remains, in law, the data controller for the purposes of the DPA 1998, subject to the legislation and the Information Commissioner's enforcement powers. Subject to overall compliance with the DPA 1998, particularly the seventh data protection principle (relating to security) and the requirement of that principle that there should be written contracts between controllers and processors, the Information Commissioner acknowledges that such transfers *can* ensure adequacy, subject to there being no *particular* risks clearly apparent in the third country in question.

The Model Contracts must be used as drafted, but companies do need to complete the blank appendices which describe such matters as the type of data and purpose of the transfer. There is little international experience on this as yet, but one could envisage a situation where a multi-national group exports all its EU data to be hosted in the US, uses the controller – processor Model Contract and is not required to file a copy in the UK under current

UK legislation, but **is** in Spain. The Spanish authority has given advice on the need for additional security for sensitive data transferred electronically. The Model Contract requires the security measures to be spelled out in an appendix. If the appendix as completed indicates a breach of the Spanish requirement, could the Spanish regulator stop transfers? It would appear so, because the Community Findings regarding Model Contracts say:

> The competent authorities in the Member States may exercise their existing powers to prohibit or suspend the data flows to third countries in order to protect individuals with regard to the processing of their personal data in cases where:
> (a) a competent authority has established that the data importer has not respected the contractual clauses in the Annex; or
> (b) there is a substantial likelihood that the standard contractual clauses in the Annex are not being or will not be complied with and the continuing transfer would create an imminent risk of grave harm to the data subjects.'

Other Community Findings

At the time of writing, five countries' laws have been approved by Community Findings as providing the necessary protection – Switzerland, Hungary, Canada (with minor limitations), Argentina and Guernsey. The Working Party has approved the Isle of Man law (so it is likely to be approved by the Committee) and is reviewing the Australian laws.

Company codes of conduct as a possible transfer mechanism

Background

Model Contracts may not be acceptable to all companies. The export may be between **branches** of the same company or offices of an international partnership, where it may be impossible, as a matter of law, to put in place binding contracts between

them. Company groups can be extremely complex, changing frequently, making the use of contracts a practical nightmare – both in ensuring all existing group members sign up and, as groups change, ensuring that all new members join the contract 'web'.

Many international groups hope to persuade national regulators that company codes of conduct (internal rules for compliance with data protection) can provide adequate protection for transfers. This is because many such groups already have (and take seriously) extensive protections for individuals created by, say, global rules on drafting privacy policies; global information security policies; global website design policies; communications monitoring policies; global HR policies and so on.

Unlike Model Contracts, individual company codes are **not** capable of being approved as a mechanism for securing 'adequacy' of transfers from any Member State.

The Working Party working document on the use of binding corporate rules for international data transfers ('the paper')

The Working Party on the protection of individuals with regard to the processing of personal data comprises representatives of the EU data protection regulators and acts as an independent adviser to the European Commission. One of its working documents, the paper (dated 3 June 2003), sets out the issues to address in creating binding corporate rules ('BCRs') likely to find favour with national regulators.

DRAFTING BCRs

The paper indicates that BCRs must comply with the following:
(1) they must be **binding or legally enforceable** to be 'sufficient safeguards' for Art 26(2). The difficult area is ensuring 'binding' BCRs. Commonly parent companies impose them on subsidiaries, but with no real sanction from a corporate perspective if subsidiaries fail to comply.

The paper acknowledges groups vary: some very close knit with all subsidiaries wholly-owned and others more diverse. It says 'for loose conglomerates, binding corporate rules are very unlikely to be a suitable tool. The diversity between their members and the broad scope of the processing activities involved would make it very difficult (if not impossible) to meet the requirements outlined in this Working Document'.

The paper says:

... it is not for the Working Party to stipulate the way in which corporate groups should guarantee that all the members are effectively bound or feel compelled by the rules, although some examples are well known such as internal policies whose application is the responsibility of the headquarters or internal codes of conduct backed by intra company agreements (ideally the binding corporate rules should be adopted by the board of directors of the ultimate parent of the group). But corporate groups must bear in mind that those applying for an authorisation will have to demonstrate to the grantor of the authorisation that this is effectively the case throughout the group.

(2) they must be **corporate**, that is rules for multinational companies, usually set up under the responsibility of the headquarters meaning a company group is effectively bound by the BCRs;

(3) they must relate to **international data transfers** – the main reason for their existence;

(4) there must be **provisions guaranteeing a good level of compliance**. An internal group privacy policy must be demonstrably known, understood and effectively applied group-wide by appropriately trained employees. The group should appoint appropriate staff, with top management support, to oversee and ensure compliance.

Clearly, this will have HR implications in terms of training and designating appropriate staff;

(5) they must be subject to **audits**. This means provision for self-audits and that the competent data protection authority ('authority') can require audit by it. There will be manpower issues, in setting up self-auditing procedures;

(6) there must be a clearly identified complaint handling department;

(7) they must provide for co-operation with authorities. Undertakings that each and every group member will accept audits and abide by the authority's advice on interpretation and application of the BCRs must be included;

(8) they must provide for liability. Data subjects covered by BCRs must become third party beneficiaries entitled to enforce compliance with BCRs by complaint to the authority or the competent court (irrespective of their nationality). This concept already exists in the Model Contracts.

Group headquarters (if EU based) or one of the European companies should accept responsibility for, and agree to take necessary remedial action for, the acts of all non-EEA group members and 'where appropriate, to pay compensation ... for any damage resulting from the violation of the binding corporate rules by any member bound by the rules'.

The EU-based entity must accept it can be **sued** in the EEA and must be prepared to compensate data subjects not satisfied with remedies from the internal complaints procedures.

Groups might have to satisfy regulators that:

(1) the EEA headquarters/European member with delegated data protection responsibilities has sufficient assets in the Community to pay compensation for BCR breaches or has taken measures to ensure this (insurance, say); and

(2) data subjects have been notified that their personal data is being communicated to non EEA members.

CO-OPERATION BETWEEN AUTHORITIES

The paper appreciates that different regulators will be approached to approve BCRs and provides for a co-operation procedure allowing companies to make one application via a single authority that it is to be hoped will, through the co-ordination process, lead to approval by other relevant authorities.

One can immediately see difficulties with this – are some Member States more pro-BCRs than others? How easy will it be for one authority to persuade another to accept such BCRs without change? How long will it take?

> If the Art 29 Working Party is adopted as a 'super-regulator' under the proposed HR Directive (see Chapter 1) it may be that it can take a role in the EU-wide approval of BCRs.

The Information Commissioner's views on BCRs

The Information Commissioner's office is being pro-active in this area working very closely with the Dutch authority, and has recently circulated a paper on how to create binding BCRs. However, BCRs are not yet commonplace, although a few have been approved in Germany and elsewhere. The Information Commissioner invites companies to talk to his office about creating BCRs.

Of particular interest to HR practitioners is the fact that the Information Commissioner expects such rules to bind employees. His guidance says: 'Employees must be bound by the rules. We suggest that this might be achieved by way of specific obligations contained in a contract of employment, by linking observance of the rules with disciplinary procedures, by arranging adequate training programmes and by providing evidence of senior staff commitment, including the title of the person ultimately responsible within the organisation for compliance'.

Conclusion

There are a number of options to enable the transfer of HR data outside the EEA and UK companies must ensure that their transfers take place in a compliant manner. The flowchart and checklist below are designed to assist in carrying out that assessment.

Transfer of data overseas – summary of main issues

1. Are you processing your HR data fairly in accordance with the first data protection principle?
2. Do you plan to export HR data from the UK?
3. Is it going outside the EEA?
4. Is it going to a country in respect of which an applicable 'Community Finding' is in place (for example to a US company that has subscribed to the 'safe harbor' or using a Model Contract) in which event the export may take place freely.
5. Is any of the data 'sensitive personal data'. Most commonly, in the HR context, this will be health data or data about racial/ethnic origin.
6. If it is sensitive personal data, can you comply with one of the conditions in DPA 1998, Sch 3 to legitimise that processing?
7. If the data is to be exported to a country where the level of protection for personal data is not adequate, how do you propose to satisfy the adequacy test?
8. If you are planning such an export, have you explained the lack of adequacy to the data subjects?
9. Have you reviewed the level of adequacy, as recommended by the Information Commissioner, and concluded that it exists? If so, the transfer can proceed (but bear in mind that the Information Commissioner could, if there are complaints about your procedures in future, conclude that the level is *not* adequate).
10. If you cannot satisfy yourself as to the level of adequacy, can you satisfy a condition in DPA 1998, Sch 4?
11. If so, which condition? If the condition is consent, are you satisfied that it has been freely given?

Cross-border transfers

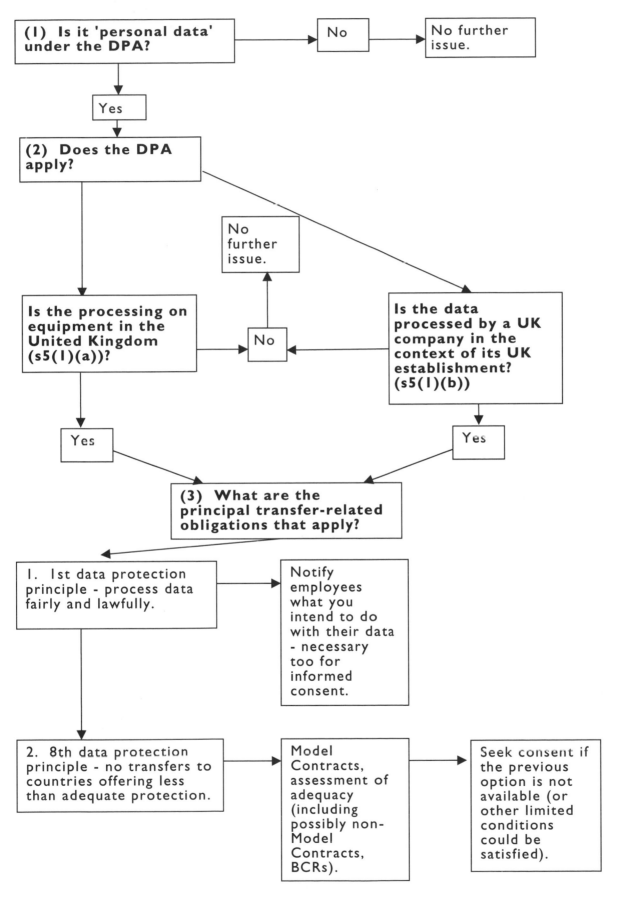

Exemptions

Helena Davies

This chapter details the various exemptions that are available to the Data Protection Act 1998 as contained in DPA 1998, ss 28 to 38 and Sch 7. Those that have most relevance in the employment context have already been discussed earlier, particularly in Chapter 4.

National security

Under DPA 1998, s 28, personal data is exempt from any of the provisions of:
* the data protection principles;
* Part II of the DPA 1998 (individuals' rights), Part III (notification) and Part V (enforcement); and

- DPA 1998, s 55 (which prohibits the unlawful obtaining of personal data)

if the data is required for the purpose of safeguarding national security (of which a certificate of exemption, signed by a Minister of the Crown, is conclusive evidence).

Crime and taxation

Under DPA 1998, s 29(1) personal data processed for any of the 'crime and taxation purposes' (ie the prevention or detection of crime; the apprehension or prosecution of offenders; or the assessment or collection of any tax or duty or any imposition of a similar nature) is exempt from:

- the first data protection principle, except that part which requires compliance with the conditions for processing (and the conditions for processing sensitive data); and
- subject access

to the extent to which the application of those provisions to the data would be likely to prejudice any of the crime and taxation purposes. In other words, the data controller must not disregard those provisions unless their application would be likely to prejudice any of the crime and taxation purposes.

Under DPA 1998, s 29(2), personal data which is processed for the purpose of discharging statutory functions and consists of information obtained for that purpose from a person who had it in his possession for any of the crime and taxation purposes, is exempt from the 'subject information provisions' (DPA 1998, Sch 1, Part II, paras 2 and 3, which refer to the provision of fair processing information and DPA 1998 s 7, subject access) to the extent to which the application of those provisions to the data would be likely to prejudice any of the crime and taxation purposes.

Under DPA 1998, s 29(3), personal data is exempt from the 'non-disclosure provisions' (ie the first data protection principle, except where it requires compliance with the conditions in DPA 1998, Schs 2 and 3; the second, third, fourth and fifth data protection principles; and DPA 1998 s 10 and s 14(1) to (3)) in any case where the disclosure is for any of the crime and taxation purposes and where the

application of those provisions in relation to the disclosure would be likely to prejudice any of the crime and taxation purposes.

As a general point, exemption from the non-disclosure provisions is available where public interest requires disclosure which might otherwise be in breach of the DPA 1998. The exemption does not provide an automatic exemption from each of the non-disclosure provisions. An exemption from the non-disclosure provisions is only from those non-disclosure provisions which would (if applied) be inconsistent with the disclosure in question.

It should be noted that the three exemptions under DPA 1998, s 29(1), (2) and (3) only apply where there is likely to be prejudice to one of the crime and taxation purposes. The Information Commissioner takes the view that, for any of these three exemptions to apply, there would have to be a substantial chance, rather than a mere risk, that in a particular case the purposes would be noticeably damaged (*Legal Guidance*, para 5.3.4).

Under DPA 1998, s 29(4), there is an exemption where personal data is processed for any of the crime and taxation purposes and:

- the data controller is a relevant authority, such as a government department; and
- the personal data consists of a classification applied to the data subject as part of a system of risk assessment operated by that authority for the assessment or collection of any tax or duty or the prevention or detection of crime relating to payments from public funds.

Where the exemption applies, personal data is exempt from the subject access provisions to the extent to which the exemption is required in the interests of the operation of the system.

Health, education and social work

DPA 1998, s 30 allows the government to exempt certain data from the subject information provisions. The Data Protection (Subject Access Modification) (Health) Order 2000 (SI 2000/413) provides for exemption from DPA 1998, s 7 (subject access) for data relating to the physical or mental health or condition of the data subject, to the extent to which the application of DPA 1998, s 7 would be likely to cause serious harm to the physical or mental health or condition of the data subject or any other person.

There are similar orders relating to education and social work records (the Data Protection (Subject Access Modifications) (Education) Order 2000 (SI 2000/414) and the Data Protection (Subject Access Modifications) (Social Work) Order 2000 (SI 2000/415)).

Regulatory activity

DPA 1998, s 31 provides an exemption from the subject information provisions for the processing of personal data by reference to numerous different categories of regulatory function exercised by public 'watchdogs' such as the Financial Services Authority or General Medical Council. The exemption is only available to the extent that the application of the provisions would be likely to prejudice the proper discharge of those functions.

Processing for special purposes

Under DPA 1998, s 32, 'special purposes' means the purposes of journalism, artistic purposes or literary purposes. There are conditions for the processing of personal data for special purposes to qualify for any exemption. These conditions are that:
- personal data is processed only for the special purposes;
- the processing is undertaken with a view to the publication by any person of any journalistic, literary or artistic material;
- the data controller reasonably believes that, taking account in particular of the special importance of the public interest in freedom of expression, publication would be in the public interest; and
- the data controller reasonably believes that, in all the circumstances, compliance with the provision in respect of which the exemption is claimed is incompatible with the special purposes.

If all the conditions are satisfied the exemption available is from:
- the data protection principles except the seventh principle; and
- DPA 1998 ss 7, 10, 12, 12A and 14(1) to (3).

Research, history and statistics

DPA 1998, s 33 provides various exemptions in respect of processing of data for research purposes provided the processing is exclusively for those purposes and that:
- the data is not processed to support measures or decisions relating to particular individuals; and
- the data is not processed in such a way that substantial damage or distress is, or is likely to be, caused to any data subject.

Where the exemption applies:
- the further processing of personal data will not be considered incompatible with the purposes for which it is obtained (for the second data protection principle);
- the personal data may be kept indefinitely despite the fifth data protection principle; and
- subject access does not have to be given provided that the results of the research or any resulting statistics are not made available in a form which identifies data subjects.

Even where the exemption applies, the data controller is still required to comply with the rest of the DPA 1998, including the first and second principles.

Information made available to the public

DPA 1998, s 34 provides that when data consists of information which the data controller is obliged by law to make available to the public, personal data is exempt from:
- the subject information provisions;
- the fourth data protection principle;
- DPA 1998, s 12A and s 14(1) to (3); and
- the non-disclosure provisions.

The exemption only applies to the information that the data controller is required to publish.

Disclosures required by law

Under DPA 1998, s 35(1), where the disclosure is required by law, personal data is exempt from the non-disclosure provisions.

Disclosures made in connection with legal proceedings

Under DPA 1998, s 35(2), where the disclosure is necessary:

- for the purposes of, or in connection with, any legal proceedings; or
- for the purpose of obtaining legal advice; or
- is otherwise necessary for the purpose of establishing, exercising or defending legal rights,

personal data is exempt from the non-disclosure provisions.

DPA 1998, Sch 2 and Sch 3 still have to be complied with.

Domestic purposes

There is a wide-ranging exemption under DPA 1998, s 36 whereby personal data is exempt from the data protection principles and the provisions of Part II (individuals' rights) and Part III (notification) of the DPA 1998 where it is processed by an individual only for the purposes of that individual's personal, family or household affairs (including recreational purposes).

Miscellaneous subject access exemptions

Under the Data Protection (Miscellaneous Subject Access Exemptions) Order 2000 (SI 2000/419) as amended, there are a number of enactments which restrict disclosure of certain personal data or information, such as adoption records. Where these

restrictions apply, the data is also exempt from DPA 1998, s 7.

Miscellaneous exemptions under DPA 1998, Sch 7

Confidential references

Personal data which consists of a confidential reference given, or to be given, by the data controller for specified purposes (education, training or employment, appointment to office or provision of any service) is exempt from subject access under DPA 1998, Sch 7, para 1.

This exemption is discussed in detail in the chapter on subject access requests.

Armed forces

Where the application of the subject information provisions to personal data would be likely to prejudice the combat effectiveness of any of the armed forces then personal data is exempt from the subject information provisions.

Judicial appointments

Personal data processed for specified purposes in relation to judicial and Crown appointments and honours is exempt from the subject information provisions.

Management forecasts and negotiations

Personal data processed for the purpose of management forecasting or management planning is exempt from the subject information provisions, to the extent to which the application of any of the subject information provisions would be likely to prejudice the conduct of the business or other activity of the data controller. Also, where personal data consists of records of the intention of the data controller in relation to any negotiations with the data subject, the personal data is exempt from the subject information provisions to the extent to which the application of those provisions would be likely to prejudice the negotiations.

This is discussed in more detail in Chapter 4.

Corporate finance

There is an exemption from the subject information provisions for personal data processed for the purposes of or in connection with a 'corporate finance service' provided by a 'relevant person' (both as defined in DPA 1998, Sch 7). The exemption is only available to the extent to which the application of the subject information provisions could (or, in the reasonable belief of the data controller, could) affect the price or value of particular instruments of a price sensitive nature, such as company shares. This

may be relevant in the context of disclosure on corporate transactions (see Chapter 6).

Legal professional privilege

If personal data consists of information in respect of which a claim to legal professional privilege could be maintained, it is exempt from the subject information provisions. This is covered in detail in the chapter on subject access requests.

Self-incrimination

If, by complying with a subject access request, a person would reveal evidence of the commission of any offence, other than an offence under the DPA 1998 or the Data Protection Act 1984, exposing him to proceedings for that offence, the person need not comply with the subject access request or order.

Chapter 9

Miscellaneous issues

Adam Turner

This chapter explores employment matters which raise important data protection issues for employers but which do not fall naturally within any of the other topics considered in this Report. In particular, the following issues are addressed:

- recruitment and selection (including vetting of employees and verification of application information)
- psychometric testing
- automated decision making
- statutory discrimination questionnaires.

Recruitment and selection

A number of data protection issues arise during the recruitment and selection process. Part I of the Employment Practices Data Protection Code (the 'Code of Practice') is specifically devoted to this area. Part I of the Code of Practice was published in March 2002 and the current Information Commissioner has confirmed that he will be reviewing it to ensure that the guidance is practical and user-friendly. At the time of writing, it is expected that the broad substance of the current version of Part I of the Code of Practice will not be significantly revised.

Although these are not expressly spelled out in the current version of Part I of the Code of Practice, certain core themes can be identified. These include:

- employers have legitimate business needs in ensuring that their recruitment and selection processes are rigorous and sufficiently comprehensive to enable them to hire the right candidates;
- applicants should be made aware of the nature and extent of the information collected in the recruitment and selection process, and the reasons for which it is held;
- applicants have legitimate expectations that they can keep their personal lives private and are entitled to a degree of privacy during the recruitment and selection process;
- if employers wish to verify an applicant's information and/or carry out vetting, they should be clear about the purpose and satisfied that this is justified by real benefits that will be delivered;
- given the extent to which personal data may be obtained from third party sources during the recruitment and selection process, care should be taken to ensure that such data is relevant and accurate. This may include giving applicants the opportunity to make representations about the data at appropriate points in the process.

Some commentators have criticised the current version of Part I of the Code of Practice as being too prescriptive. Despite this, it does set out clearly the various data protection issues arising in this context and so is recommended reading.

The Code of Practice usefully divides the recruitment and selection process into different stages, namely advertising, applications, verification, short-listing, interviews, pre-employment vetting and retention of recruitment records.

The following highlights the more important issues employers should bear in mind in this context.

Advertising

- Job advertisements should identify the name of the organisation to which the applicant will be providing his personal data. If the employer does not wish to be named at the advertising stage, it should usually identify itself on the application form.
- If the employer does not wish to be named at the application stage (which may be the case where an intermediary such as a recruitment agency is involved) the applicant should be told this and also told the identity of the recruiting employer at the earliest opportunity.
- The purposes for which information will be used should be explained, save to the extent that this is self-evident.

Applications

- Employers should tailor the application form so that it only asks for relevant information. This is especially so where sensitive personal data is being requested.
- Obtain the applicant's explicit consent where sensitive personal data is needed. This may be the case, for example, where information is requested about marital status or criminal convictions, or where drug testing is carried out. Remember that to be valid, such consent must be given freely and the applicant should be told clearly what personal data is involved and how it will be used (see Chapter 1).

Where an employer seeks information which is held by third parties, the latter may require proof that the applicant has consented before releasing the information to the employer. Where this is the case it is sensible to ask the applicant to give such additional consents, even where sensitive personal data is not involved. This can be done, for example, by tailoring the application form as necessary.

Employers often receive unsolicited applications 'on spec'. Although, strictly, to comply with the first data protection principle an employer should respond with a notice detailing how it might process the data, in practice this is not necessary, provided the employer deals with the application in a reasonably anticipated manner, such as progressing the application to the next stage of the recruitment process or keeping the information on file for a short period in case any suitable vacancies arise. However, any unexpected use, such as an intention to retain the application for a longer period or to send it on to other group companies whether in the UK or elsewhere, should be notified to the individual.

Verification

Verification is the process of checking that details supplied by applicants are accurate and complete. Employers should only go so far as is necessary to check information that is requested as part of the application process.

- Applicants should be informed of the scope of the verification process and how this is carried out, if this has not previously been done.
- Where verification highlights discrepancies with information supplied by the applicant, fair processing will include giving the applicant an opportunity to make representations about the discrepancies.

Short-listing

Employers will obviously have processes in place to reduce the pool of applicants as the recruitment process goes on. For example, it is becoming increasingly common to make use of psychometric analysis or other testing to 'narrow the field'.

The use of psychometric testing gives rise to a number of data protection issues. These are explored in the section on 'Psychometric testing' below.

Psychometric or other testing will often involve an automated decision-making process. Where automated processing is used as the sole means of determining who goes through to the next stage, the DPA 1998 provides additional rights for the applicant, including rights to have this automated decision revisited. Further details are set out below in the section on 'Automated processing'.

Employers should take steps to ensure that any form of short-listing and selection process is applied in a way which is consistent and fair to all applicants.

Interviews

Notes or even video/audio recordings may be taken at interview. Employers need to ensure that their overall document retention policies take into account such personal data obtained during the recruitment and selection process. Save in relation to the successful applicant, organisations should usually only keep recruitment and selection information for a limited period. Further information on document retention periods can be found in the section on 'Retention and destruction of records' in Chapter 2.

Pre-employment vetting

In some circumstances, it may be appropriate for employers to conduct further background checks above and beyond the verification checks mentioned above.

- Given the importance of an individual's rights of privacy in this context, employers should usually only carry out pre-employment vetting where the job involves an area of special risk, for example where it includes working with children or vulnerable adults.
- If vetting is required, an employer should attempt to use the least intrusive method of obtaining information.
- Applicants should be told how and when vetting will occur as early as possible during the

recruitment process – ideally at the application stage.

- Blanket vetting will almost always be unacceptable. Vetting should be targeted only at successful candidates in order to obtain specific information. Accordingly, vetting is likely to be carried out late in the recruitment and selection process.

Even in situations where an employer feels it has legitimate reasons for carrying out vetting, for example where it has a history of drug misuse in its workforce, it is unlikely to be proportionate for the employer to introduce blanket vetting (such as drug testing and police checks) on all potential recruits. Vetting often involves the processing of data about a person's health, as to which see the section on 'Medical testing' in Chapter 3.

- Employers should usually only request information about criminal convictions if necessary. When the Criminal Records Bureau is fully operational, it will be a criminal offence to require an individual to access his criminal record as part of the recruitment process. Further information can be found in the section on 'Treatment of criminal information' in Chapter 2.
- Applicants should be given the opportunity to respond to any issues arising from the vetting process which might affect their recruitment prospects.

Recruitment agencies

Many employers use recruitment agencies to find suitable applicants. Where an agency is involved, the employer acts as a data controller with overall responsibility for such personal data and the recruitment agency is a data processor (although in some circumstances the agency may also act in the capacity of a data controller). Detail on the respective duties of data controllers and data processors can be found in Chapter 1.

Given the employer's role as the data controller, it should ensure that the agency complies with data protection requirements in respect of the information the agency processes on the employer's behalf. This will include:

- putting in place a written data processing agreement with the agency (in accordance with the seventh data protection principle and DPA 1998, Sch 1, paras 11 and 12). The agreement should include provisions setting out (broadly) how compliance with the DPA 1998 will be achieved. This will include clauses relating to security measures, uses of data, retention times and so on. For more detail, see the section on 'Data processors' in Chapter 1;
- checking that the agency obtains the necessary consents from applicants in respect of sensitive personal data.

An agency is required (as from 6 April 2004) under reg 29 of the Conduct of Employment Agencies and Employment Business Regulations 2003 (SI 2003/3319) to keep certain records for a minimum of one year. As this length of time will usually be longer than the period specified in the employer's own policy for retention of records of unsuccessful candidates, the data processing agreement should usually require the agency to keep the records for no longer than this statutory minimum period.

Further information on document retention can be found in Chapter 2.

Psychometric testing

What is psychometric testing?

Psychometric testing is helpfully defined by the CIPD in its 'Psychological Testing – Quick Facts' guide (available from www.cipd.co.uk) as 'tests which can be systematically scored and administered, which are used to measure individual differences (for example in personality, aptitude, ability, attainment or intelligence). [These tests] are supported by a body of evidence and statistical data which demonstrates their validity.'

Psychometric testing in the employment context

Psychometric testing is being used increasingly by employers, typically at the recruitment stage, as one of the selection tools for identifying the successful candidate. For example, personality tests might be used to highlight areas to explore further at the interview stage; if the tests show a desire to work alone rather than as part of a team, the candidate may be questioned to determine whether this represents a rounded picture of their attitude and methods of working.

Although psychometric testing most often features during the recruitment process, it can also be used at other times during the employment relationship, for example in order to assess the development needs of the workforce to make promotion decisions, or in the context of a redundancy selection exercise.

The test results and the reports which are produced in light of such testing will usually be personal data which is subject to the requirements of the DPA 1998. In some circumstances, psychometric testing data might include sensitive personal data to the extent that it gives information on an individual's mental health, although it should be rare for employers to test for such information. Where, however, sensitive personal data is collected the usual additional safeguards under the DPA 1998 will be relevant, as to which see the section on 'DPA 1998, Sch 3 conditions' in Chapter 1.

Employers need to bear in mind a number of issues when carrying out psychometric testing. These include:
- identifying the qualities needed for the position, so as to ensure that the psychometric testing is properly focused. The particular emphasis here is on the second data protection principle, namely that employers should not collect more information than is properly needed for the purpose(s) at hand;
- tests should be carried out in a way which is objective, consistent and fair to all individuals (the first data protection principle). In addition, care should be taken to ensure that the testing does not discriminate unlawfully against any particular classes of applicant. Tests which do so discriminate against a particular individual or a prohibited group will breach the first principle

of the DPA 1998, as the data will not be processed lawfully;

The British Psychological Society (BPS) offers good practice guidelines for employers to help them ensure that the testing process is carried out fairly. Adherence to guidelines produced by this body or by any other similarly recognised organisation in this field should in practice mean that employers will comply with their obligations under the first principle of the DPA 1998.

- ensure that the people administering the tests and interpreting the results are properly qualified to do so;

The BPS, for example, offers a qualification scheme in relation to the administration of psychometric tests which is a generally accepted industry standard. Accordingly, it should be safe for employers to use administrators who have the appropriate BPS qualifications. Indeed, many test providers require evidence that the tests will be administered by properly qualified people before agreeing to sell the tests to employers.

- the individuals taking the tests should be given certain information prior to doing so. Much of this information may have been supplied already, for example earlier in the recruitment process. However, to the extent that this has not been done, the individual should be given the identity of the employer and told the purpose(s) for which his data is being processed (for example, in order to produce a report which will assist the employer in making the recruitment decision). Where test results are analysed by a third party, this should also be identified;
- third parties administering the tests will be data processors. In light of this, employers, as data controllers, must ensure that they comply with their obligations under the seventh data protection principle. For more details on the issues associated with using data processors, see Chapter 1;
- there is a progression towards using the internet or other long-distance media (for example fax back services) for the purposes of carrying out psychometric tests. In addition to the issues of security raised by the seventh data protection principle, to the extent that data is transferred

outside the EEA employers should be aware of their obligations under the eighth principle of the DPA 1998. Further information on this topic can be found in Chapter 7 on the transfer of data overseas.

Automated processing

The DPA 1998 includes specific provisions giving an individual additional rights in situations where significant decisions are made in relation to him solely by reference to the automatic processing of his personal data.

DPA 1998, s 12(1) provides:

> An individual is entitled at any time, by notice in writing to any data controller, to require the data controller to ensure that no decision taken by or on behalf of the data controller which significantly affects that individual is based solely on the processing by automatic means of personal data in respect of which that individual is the data subject for the purpose of evaluating matters relating to him such as, for example, his performance at work, his creditworthiness, his reliability or his conduct.

As can be seen, a number of criteria need to be satisfied before DPA 1998, s 12 applies, and in particular the following:

- the processing must be of automated (electronic) data, not manual data;
- the decision must be based **solely** on the automated processing – where the automated processing simply provides information which is one factor among many used in the decision-making process, DPA 1998, s 12 will not apply;
- the decision must have a significant effect on the individual (for example, whether or not the individual goes through to the next stage of the recruitment process);
- the decision must relate to matters such as the individual's performance at work, his reliability or his conduct. This requirement highlights that the right can apply to employment decisions taken at various stages of the employment relationship.

In the employment context, as mentioned earlier, automated processing is most often relevant where some form of testing is carried out such as psychometric testing. This will most often arise during the recruitment and selection process, but may be relevant in other situations, for example when a company uses such testing as part of its redundancy or promotion selection process.

A recent example of the impact of automated processing in the employment context is the story of Carl Filer and his engagement to work as a salesman at B&Q's Bournemouth branch in early 2001. Contrary to the company's usual recruitment procedure, Mr Filer was hired without completing a psychometric test. He was very quickly singled out as a peak performer with good promotion prospects. Mr Filer subsequently took the test, which he failed. As a result, he was dismissed.

What rights do employees have when DPA 1998, s 12 applies?

- An employee can serve notice in writing to the employer requiring the employer to ensure that no decison is taken which satisfies the criteria mentioned above (DPA 1998, s 12(1)). In practice it is very uncommon for employers to receive such a notice.
- Where automated decisions falling within DPA 1998, s 12(1) are made, the employer must, as soon as reasonably practicable, give a notice to the employee telling him that the decision was taken on that basis. The employee then has 21 days from receiving the notice to send a counter-notice in writing requiring the employer to reconsider the decision or take a new decision on a different basis. The employer has a further 21 days from receipt of the counter-notice to send a further written notice specifying the steps that he intends to take to comply with the employee's notice (DPA 1998, s 12(2) and (3)).

Certain decisions are exempt from the above rights (DPA 1998, s 12(4) and (5)). In the employment arena these will mostly be decisions taken for the purposes of recruitment, or in the course of employment, in either case where the decision grants the employee's request or where steps have been taken to safeguard the employee's legitimate interests (for example by giving him the opportunity to make representations).

It is good data protection practice in any event to give employees the opportunity to make representations in relation to matters involving automated processing.

Practical steps for employers in light of automated processing rights

- Consider whether decision-making solely on the basis of automated processing is appropriate. It is more common for employers to use the results of automated testing as one of many factors in reaching their decision.
- Put in place a system to notify individuals when automated decision making is part of the relevant process such as a recruitment process, preferably before such decisions are made but in any event no later than is reasonably practicable after the decision.
- Have in place a back-up (manual) decision-making system to deal with situations where an individual exercises his DPA 1998, s 12 rights.

Discrimination questionnaires

Background

All existing strands of discrimination law include a questionnaire procedure. This procedure is designed to enable individuals who believe that they might have a complaint of discrimination to obtain information from their employers so that they can clarify the situation and, if necessary, raise the issue with the employer and/or bring a claim.

Employers need to bear in mind their data protection obligations when replying to a questionnaire served under any of the actionable strands of discrimination. The data protection issues associated with such questionnaires have most obviously been brought into sharp relief in the context of equal pay claims. This may be because, first, by their very nature the

main focus of equal pay questionnaires is to obtain personal data on the remuneration of other staff; and secondly, the equal pay questionnaire procedure was only recently introduced (in April 2003) at a time when data protection issues have been very much at the forefront of people's minds.

For ease of reference, the following analysis assumes that an employer is dealing with an equal pay questionnaire. However, similar principles apply to all the strands of discrimination.

A copy of the standard equal pay questionnaire and reply form has been published for use by the employee raising the equal pay issue (the complainant) and by the employer and can be downloaded from the Women and Equality Unit website (www.womenandequalityunit.gov.uk). The equal pay standard forms come with brief guidance notes and further advice is available from the Equal Opportunities Commission's website (www.eoc.org.uk).

Employers are given an eight-week time limit to reply to an equal pay questionnaire. (This time limit is being introduced as a standard response time across all the discrimination strands, although at the time of writing there are still variations across some of the strands.)

Although employers are not legally obliged to reply, failure to do so without reasonable excuse within this timeframe entitles an employment tribunal to draw any inference it considers just and equitable. The same is also true where an employer does reply, but is evasive or equivocal when doing so.

The main data protection issue for employers here is compliance with the first data protection principle – personal data must be processed fairly and carefully and not at all unless one of the conditions in DPA 1998, Sch 2 (or in the case of sensitive personal data, DPA 1998, Sch 3) are met. The DPA 1998, Sch 2 conditions which are relevant here are either obtaining the consent of the comparator to the disclosure of his information (DPA 1998, Sch 2, para 1) or claiming that such disclosure falls within the 'legitimate interest' provision (DPA 1998, Sch 2, para 6). Claiming the legitimate interest condition is not as easy as it first sounds; this requires an employer to balance its and the complainant's interests with those of the potential comparator. In this context the employer's duty of fairness under the first principle is primarily going to be towards the potential comparator. This is because an employer's duty under the first principle is to the 'data subject' and in the context of a request for comparator data the data subject will be the comparator. Accordingly, if the comparator objects to the disclosure of his personal information, it is unlikely that the legitimate interest provision will be satisfied if the employer does then fully disclose it.

The law of confidence

At least some of the information requested in an equal pay questionnaire may be confidential, for example details of a possible comparator's salary. Although such information is not sensitive personal data, it is still usually considered information of a very private quality.

Whilst it is unclear, there are arguments that disclosure of such information might amount to a breach of confidence. If breach of confidence is an issue and the employer does commit such a breach by disclosing the information, the employer will be acting unlawfully. Acting unlawfully will mean that the employer is in breach of the first data protection principle in any event.

How then can an employer deal with these issues?

Seek consent

This is one situation where obtaining the consent of the potential comparator is the most sensible first step.

Fair processing will require employers to inform the potential comparator in any event that the complainant has requested such disclosure (see Part 2 of the Code of Practice, section 11). It will be uncommon for employers to have included reference to such processing in any general purpose statement already given to its workforce. This means the employer should be liaising with the potential comparator anyway, so it can easily take that opportunity also to ask for his consent to disclosure. Obtaining consent has the additional benefit of avoiding breach of confidence issues.

To deal with this situation, employers may wish to create a standard 'consent form' to give to the potential comparator, which explains the situation and asks whether the comparator is willing to have his personal data disclosed. An example consent form for questionnaires is set out in Appendix K.

Where consent is not forthcoming

Where consent is not forthcoming, an employer should not feel that it is 'off the hook'. True, it is now more difficult to comply with its data protection and any confidentiality obligations, but in order to avoid the drawing of adverse inferences by a tribunal the employer should still aim to answer the questions as fully as it can.

- Employers who feel unable to answer a questionnaire fully (or at all) should state their reasons why in their reply – the existing discrimination questionnaires include a provision expressly inviting employers to do this.

- Where possible, disclose the information in anonymised form. By doing this, the information will not be personal data (and the DPA 1998 will not apply) and there will be no breach of confidence if it is not possible to identify the individual whose data has been disclosed.

- If it is not suitable to anonymise the information, try dealing with the request in general terms, for example, by confirming that a comparator's pay is above a certain rate.

- When replying to a questionnaire, employers should also ask the complainant to give a confidentiality undertaking under which he agrees not to use the information other than for the purposes of his equal pay enquiry. If considered appropriate, it might even be suitable to ask the complainant to return all such information once the issue has been resolved. Where an employment tribunal has ordered disclosure (see below) the employer need not seek any such undertaking, as the employment tribunal rules mirror the provisions of the Civil Procedure Rules 31.22 which provide that a party to whom a document has been disclosed may use it only for the purposes of the proceedings in which it is disclosed.

- Once a claim has been lodged at the employment tribunal, the tribunal has the power to order disclosure. Where it makes such an order, an employer will definitely satisfy DPA 1998, Sch 2; the employer is complying with a legal obligation to disclose the information, and therefore satisfies Sch 2, para 3.

Employers will still usually have concerns about revealing confidential information, even where they are ordered by the employment tribunal to make disclosure. Confidentiality in itself is not a basis for refusing disclosure of relevant documentation when an order has been made. However, the employment tribunal should take into account issues of confidentiality when making its order, for example by suggesting special measures such as redaction or anonymising the data.

Miscellaneous – summary of main issues

- Best practice in relation to recruitment and selection is set out in Part 1 of the Code of Practice.
- If psychometric testing is used in the recruitment process (or at some later stage in the employment relationship) care needs to be taken to ensure the testing is conducted in a fair, objective way and that the results are directly relevant and necessary to the recruitment (or other) decision.
- Where a significant decision is taken about an employee solely by automated means an employer should ensure that at the very least a mechanism is in place allowing review of the decision where the employee requests it.
- In answering discrimination questionnaires employers need to bear in mind not only the rights of the person serving the questionnaire but also other individuals whose rights under the DPA 1998 or common law may be infringed by a response.

The *Durant* case: the Information Commissioner's paper

The *Durant* case and its impact on the interpretation of the Data Protection Act 1998

In the recent case of *Durant v Financial Services Authority* [2003] EWCA Civ 1746, [2003] All ER (D) 124 (Dec) (Court of Appeal (Civil Division), decision of Auld, Mummery and Buxton LJJ), the Court of Appeal considered four important issues of law concerning the right of access to personal data. (A full text of the judgment is available from the Court Service website at www.courtservice.gov.uk.) To the extent that the judgment provides clarity on these issues and reiterates the fundamental link between data protection and privacy rights it is welcomed by the Information Commissioner. This paper focuses on what the Commissioner considers to be the two most important of the issues considered by the Court, namely:

1. What makes 'data' 'personal' within the meaning of 'personal data'? and
2. What is meant by a 'relevant filing system'?

This document is aimed in particular at specialist data protection officers and professional advisers.

What 'data' are 'personal' for the purposes of the Data Protection Act 1998 ('the DPA 1998')

The DPA 1998 applies only to 'personal data' and therefore a clear understanding of what is meant by this term is essential for compliance with its provisions. The Court of Appeal concluded that:

'personal data' 'is information that affects [a person's] privacy, whether in his personal or family life, business or professional capacity'.

The concept of privacy is therefore clearly central to the definition of personal data. This suggests to the Commissioner that you should take into account whether or not the information in question is capable of having an adverse impact on the individual. The Court identified two notions that may assist in determining whether information 'is information that affects [an individual's] privacy':

The first is whether the information is biographical in a significant sense, that is, going beyond the recording of [the individual's] involvement in a matter or an event which has no personal connotations ...'

The second concerns focus. 'The information should have the [individual] as its focus rather than some other person with whom he may have been involved or some transaction or event in which he may have figured or have had an interest ...

In the *Durant* case the Court of Appeal did not consider the issue of the identifiability of an individual in the definition of 'personal data' set out in DPA 1998, s 1(1). This is often the starting point in developing an understanding of personal data. Instead, the Court of Appeal in this case concentrated on the meaning of 'relate to' in that definition, identifiability not being an issue in the case.

Where an individual's name appears in information the name will only be 'personal data' where its inclusion in the information affects the named individual's privacy. Simply because an individual's name appears on a document, the information contained in that document will not necessarily be personal data about the named individual.

It is more likely that an individual's name will be 'personal data' where the name appears together with other information about the named individual such as address, telephone number (see European Court of Justice decision in *Bodil Lindqvist v Kammaraklagaren* C-101/01, [2003] All ER (D) 77 (Nov) para 27, as referred to in para 28 of the *Durant* judgment) or information regarding his hobbies (see *Lindqvist* case (above), para 27, and *Durant* at para 28).

Provided the information in question can be linked to an identifiable individual the following are examples of personal data:
- information about the medical history of an individual;
- an individual's salary details;
- information concerning an individual's tax liabilities;
- information comprising an individual's bank statements; and
- information about individuals' spending preferences.

These types of information may be contrasted with the following examples of information which will not normally be personal data:
- mere reference to a person's name where the name is not associated with any other personal information;
- incidental mention in the minutes of a business meeting of an individual's attendance at that meeting in an official capacity; or
- where an individual's name appears on a document or email indicating only that it has been sent or copied to that particular individual, the content of that document or email does not amount to personal data about the individual unless there is other information about the individual within it.

The following comments of Auld LJ indicate some practical implications of the Court of Appeal's interpretation of 'personal data':
- 'not all information retrieved from a computer search against an individual's name or unique identifier is personal data';
- '[DPA 1998, s 7] is not an automatic key to any information, readily accessible or not, of matters in which [the party making the request for information] may be named or involved';
- 'the mere fact that a document is retrievable by reference to [the applicant for information's] name does not entitle him to a copy of it under the Act'.

Information that has as its focus something other than the individual will not be 'personal data'. For example, information that focuses on a property (for instance a structural survey) is not 'personal data', nor is information about the performance of an office department or a branch of a chain of stores. While such information may include information 'about' an individual, where the focus of the information is something other than the individual, such information will not 'relate to' the individual and, therefore, is not personal data.

However, there are many circumstances where information, for example about a house or a car, could be personal data because that information is directly linked to an individual. One example would be a valuation of a house where this was being used in order to determine the assets of a particular individual in a matrimonial dispute. Another example would be the details of a car photographed by a speed camera where those details are used to direct a notice of intention to prosecute to the registered keeper of the vehicle.

Manual files covered by the DPA 1998

The DPA 1998 only applies to 'personal data'. 'Data' as defined by the DPA 1998 includes both information held on computer and manual information provided the manual data is organised into a 'relevant filing system'. (A 'relevant filing system' is defined in the DPA 1998, s 1(1) as 'any set of information relating to individuals to the extent that, although the information is not processed by means of equipment operating automatically in response to instructions given for that purpose, the set is structured either by reference to the individual or to criteria relating to individuals, in such a way that specific information relating to a particular individual is readily accessible'.)

In the *Durant* case the Court of Appeal took the view that the Act intended to cover manual files 'only if they are of sufficient sophistication to provide the same or similar ready accessibility as a computerised filing system'.

Any manual filing system 'which, for example, requires the searcher to leaf through files to see what and whether information qualifying as personal data of the person who has made the request [for access to his personal data] is to be found there, would bear no resemblance to a computerised search.' It would not, therefore, qualify as a relevant filing system.

The judgment concluded that:

> a 'relevant filing system' for the purposes of the DPA 1998, is limited to a system:
> 1. in which the files forming part of it are structured or referenced in such a way as to clearly indicate at the outset of the search whether specific information capable of amounting to personal data of an individual requesting it under DPA 1998, s 7 is held within the system and, if so, in which file or files it is held; and
> 2. which has, as part of its own structure or referencing mechanism, a sufficiently sophisticated and detailed means of readily indicating whether and where in an individual file or files specific criteria or information about the applicant can be readily located.

The judgment includes some helpful statements as to the effect of this interpretation as follows:
- 'the protection given by the legislation is for the privacy of personal data, not documents';
- 'if the [DPA 1998] statutory scheme [for the handling of manual personal data] is to have any sensible and practical effect, it can only be in the context of filing systems that enable identification of relevant information with a minimum of time and costs, through clear referencing mechanisms within any filing system potentially containing personal data';

- 'to qualify [as a relevant filing system] under ... the Act ... requires ... a file to which [a] search [for personal data] leads to be so structured and/or indexed as to enable easy location within it or any sub-files of specific information about the data subject that he has requested'; and
- '... it is only to the extent that manual filing systems are broadly equivalent to computerised systems in ready accessibility to ... personal data that they are within the system of data protection'.

In the Information Commissioner's view it follows, therefore, that when a subject access request is received for information held in manual form (other than information contained in an 'accessible record') the statutory right to be given access to personal data will only apply if the filing system is structured as a 'relevant filing system'. ('Accessible records' are records relating to health, education and certain other accessible public records. See s 68 and DPA 1998, Sch 12 for further information.) That is to say, the filing system is structured in such a way as to allow the recipient of the request to:

Either:

a.

- know that there is a system in place which will allow the retrieval of file/s in the name of an individual (if such file/s exists); and
- know that the file/s will contain the category of personal data requested (if such data exists); or

b.

- know that there is a system in place which will allow the retrieval of file/s covering topics about individuals (for example personnel type topics such as leave, sick notes, contracts and so on); and
- know that the file/s are indexed/structured to allow the retrieval of information about a specific individual (if such information exists) (for example the topic file is subdivided in alphabetical order of individuals' names).

Where manual files fall within the definition of relevant filing system, the content will either be so sub-divided as to allow the searcher to go straight to the correct category and retrieve the information requested without a manual search, or will be so indexed as to allow a searcher to go directly to the relevant page/s.

For example, a set of legal files containing files divided into sections for legal aid, pleadings, orders, correspondence by year, instructions to counsel, counsel's advice, will not be a relevant filing system because the divisions/ referencing do not assist a searcher in retrieving the required personal information without the need to leaf through the file contents.

It is important to note that the Freedom of Information Act 2000 ('FOIA 2000') will, in 2005, amend the DPA 1998 to expand the definition of 'data'. As a result of the expanded definition, public sector bodies caught by FOIA 2000 must ensure that the personal data they hold (including unstructured manual personal data **except** unstructured manual personnel records) must be accurate, up-to-date and accessible under DPA 1998, s 7. They should also note that the compensation and rectification provisions of the DPA 1998 will apply in respect of such data although so far as subject access fees are concerned, the charges under the FOIA 2000 will apply. FOIA 2000 does not cover private or voluntary sector bodies save where they carry out public functions for a public sector body. For further information on the impact of FOIA 2000 on the meaning of 'personal data' see 'Freedom of Information Act 2000: An Introduction' available from the Commissioner's website at www.informationcommissioner.gov.uk. Also, see 'FOI Awareness Guidance No 1 on Personal Information' which can also be found on the Commissioners website. The relevant provisions of the FOIA 2000, amending the DPA 1998, are ss 68 to 73 inclusive and Sch 6.

Where information is filed in a system using individuals' names as file names, the system may not qualify as a relevant filing system if the indexing/referencing/sub-division is structured otherwise than to allow the retrieval of personal data without leafing through the file.

A filing system containing files about individuals, or topics about individuals, where the content of each file is structured purely in chronological order **will not be a relevant filing system** as the files are not appropriately structured/indexed/divided or referenced to allow the retrieval of personal data without leafing through the file.

Personnel files and other manual files using individuals' names or unique identifiers as the file names, which are sub-divided/indexed to allow retrieval of personal data without a manual search (such as, sickness, absence, contact details etc., are likely to be held in a 'relevant filing system' for the purposes of the DPA 1998. However, following the *Durant* judgment it is likely that **very few manual files will be covered by the provisions of the DPA 1998.** Most information about individuals held in manual form does not, therefore, fall within the data protection regime.

Information Commissioner's Office

02/02/04

Frequently Asked Questions and Answers (relevant filing systems)

Q1 All the information I have on file is held in chronological order with no other indexing or sub-division, how does the DPA 1998 impact on me?

A1 The information you hold in manual form is not held in a 'relevant filing system' and is therefore not 'personal data' for the purposes of the DPA 1998. Don't forget, however, that if you hold information on computer, such as the electronic versions of manual documents held on manual files, such information may be covered by the DPA 1998.

Q2 Is there any rule of thumb I can apply to establish whether I have a relevant filing system?

A2 Yes, you can apply the 'temp test'. If you employed a temporary administrative assistant (a temp), would they be able to extract specific information about an individual without any particular knowledge of your type of work or the documents you hold?

The 'temp test' assumes that the temp in question is reasonably competent, requiring only a short induction, explanation and/or operating manual on the particular filing system in question for them to be able to use it.

The temp test would not apply if any in-depth knowledge of your custom and practice is required, whether of your type of work, of the documents you hold or of any unusual features of your system, before a temp is, as a matter of practice, capable of operating the system. In such cases the system would not be a relevant filing system.

Example

John Smith is your employee. He requests details of the leave he has taken in the last six months. You have a collection of personnel files.

a   If there is a file entitled 'leave' containing alphabetical dividers the temp would have no difficulty in finding the leave record of John Smith behind the 'S' divider. **This is a relevant filing system.**

b.   If there is a file entitled 'John Smith' which is sub-divided into categories such as 'contact details', 'sickness', 'pension' and 'leave' the temp would have no difficulty in finding the leave record of John Smith. **This is a relevant filing system.**

c.   If there is a file entitled 'John Smith' in a system that only contains the leave record of employees, with leave recorded on standard forms filed in date order within the respective files for each employee, the temp would have no difficulty in finding the record of John Smith's leave taken. **This is a relevant filing system.**

d.   If there is a file entitled 'John Smith' but there is no sub-division of its contents, documents are randomly dropped into the file or are filed in chronological order regardless of the subject matter, the temp would have to leaf through the file contents to obtain the information required. **This is not a relevant filing system.**

e.   If there is a file entitled 'John Smith' with sub-dividers that classify the contents of the file in a vague or ambiguous way, (such as 'correspondence', 'comments' and 'miscellaneous'), established members of staff only know through experience and knowledge of the particular practice and custom of filing in that system that, for example, leave details are recorded on the back page of a report that is filed in the 'miscellaneous' section.

However, the temp would have to leaf through the file contents to obtain the information required because it is not clear from the structure of the file, or from any operating manual where the relevant information will be held. That would only become clear were the temp provided with additional information specific to that particular workplace and system. **This is not a relevant filing system.**

Quick guide to understanding the DPA 1998 definition of 'relevant filing systems'

1. Does your filing system contain information about individuals?
   Yes –   go to Q. 2.
   No –   you **do not** have a 'relevant filing system'.
2. Does the filing system use the names of individuals (or another unique identifier) as the file name?
   Yes –   go to Q. 4.
   No –   go to Q. 3.
3. Does the filing system use criteria relating to individuals (for example sickness absence, pensions, or qualifications) as the file name?
   Yes –   go to Q.4.
   No –   you **do not** have a 'relevant filing system'.
4. Is the information in your files held solely in chronological order?
   Yes –   you **do not** have a 'relevant filing system'.
   No –   go to Q. 5.
5. Is the content of your files indexed or subdivided to allow direct access to specific information about the individual?
   Yes –   you are likely to have a 'relevant filing system'.
   No –   you **do not** have a 'relevant filing system'.

Sample purpose statement for a company operating in the UK

(1)Notice and consent for processing of employee data

[Name of Company]

The Company values the privacy of its employees. We have therefore prepared this statement outlining our practices in relation to the collection and use of information about you.

We will endeavour to process any personal information relating to you fairly and lawfully, in accordance with the Data Protection Act 1998. We will also endeavour to comply with the Information Commissioner's Employment Practices Code of Practice.

(2)Collection of information

Good employment practice and the efficient running of our business require us to hold certain personal details about you. For example, the Company may hold your bank account details in order to pay your salary. These personal details may include sensitive personal information about you such as information on your health, racial or ethnic origin, or marital status. We obtain personal information about you from a number of sources including the application form you completed when you applied to join us, from interview notes and from details you subsequently give us. We also obtain information from other internal sources and in some cases, from external sources.

(3)Use of information

As your employer, the Company is permitted by law to use, hold or disclose personal data about you in certain circumstances, particularly where it is necessary for the performance of your employment contract or where the processing of the information is in the Company's legitimate interests. The Company is also permitted to use, hold or disclose sensitive personal data (for example about your health) if it does so because of a legal right or obligation placed on the Company (for example for disability or insurance purposes). None of these uses requires your consent.

The personal information we hold is used only for employee administration and management purposes, such as payroll administration, compilation of employee directories, performance appraisal, compensation and benefits planning, entitlement to pension, social security, life insurance or other benefits and compliance with various reporting or disclosure obligations.

The Company may disclose your personal information to contractors that perform business, administrative and management functions for the Company, in which case such contractors are required to maintain appropriate privacy safeguards. The Company may also disclose personal information to prospective purchasers, who would also be required to maintain appropriate privacy safeguards, on a sale of a part or all of the business. The Company does not disclose your personal information to third parties unless you consent to the disclosure or the disclosure is required by applicable laws, court orders or regulations.

You may also have provided the Company with information about your dependants, relatives and friends for health and other insurance policies and in connection with emergency contact details. In so far as practicable, the same protections and rights extended to the information about you are extended to the information about your dependants, relatives and friends.

(4) Retention of information

We will not retain information relating to you longer than is necessary for the purpose(s) for which it is obtained. Details of the document retention policy observed by the Company are available from the Human Resources Department.

(5) Accuracy of information

We make every effort to ensure that the information we hold about you is accurate and, where necessary, kept up to date. In the absence of evidence to the contrary we will assume that the information you provide us with is accurate. Should you inform us or we otherwise become aware of any inaccuracies in the information, they will be promptly rectified by us.

(6) Access to information

You have the right to reasonable access to your personal information maintained by the Company and the right to correct such information, as appropriate. Please contact Human Resources for further information.

Subject access requests: where to search?

Source	Subsets?	Search Issues	Policy Issues
Centrally held Human Resources Records	Personnel File		It is particularly important to ensure that personnel records are relevant and up to date. It can be embarrassing (and potentially lead to expensive litigation) if these files contain out of date and unnecessary information.
	Sickness Records		
	Health and Safety Records		
	Payroll Records		Consider implementing a policy of not supplying payroll information as this information will usually already have been supplied to the employee during employment.
	Career Development Profiles		
Email	Inbox/Sent Items/Deleted Items/Personal Folders	Whose email is to be searched? Just the person making the request or other individuals – such as line management?

Is the whole system to be searched or is it limited by date?

What search strings are to be used? Just the person's name or combinations of first/surname/initials/nickname?

Do people keep 'folders' of information? If so, how is this to be dealt with in relation to search policy? | As a starting point, consider limiting the number of individuals whose email systems will be searched.

Consider also limiting the maximum time period which will be searched (such as a specified number of months or years) |

Source	Subsets?	Search Issues	Policy Issues
	Back up archive tapes	What sort of cost and time is involved in restoring back up tapes of email so that they can be searched?	As a starting point, consider imposing a limit on the number of 'restores' which will be undertaken in response to any particular request.
Other electronic systems	Intranet	Is personal information held on the company's intranet? For example, are there mini-biographies, contact details or photographs of employees?	
	Word processing files	Are there memos or other documents about employees on the WP system? If so, how can this be searched? What search strings should be used – similar to email?	
	Other electronic files?		
Other manual files	Expenses claims		Consider a policy of not disclosing these items on the basis that the employee has already received copies.
	Files held by line management?	Only covered if they are part of a 'relevant filing system'. That is, a file constructed with reference to a particular employee or a number of employees where specific information about the person making the request could easily be located – for example cardboard dividers in a lever arch file relating to an employee separating their records into sub-sections.	
	Other manual files?		

Sample letter where subject access request is defective in some way

Ms E Hollaway
42 Cherry Orchard
Appleby
Dorset

Dear Emma

Your access request

Thank you for your letter of 14 February 2004 requesting access to the personal data which Bradshaw & Co holds about you, under the Data Protection Act 1998.

[The cheque for £10 referred to in your letter was not in fact enclosed. Please forward this to me as soon as possible. I will not be able to deal with your request until it is received.]

[Unfortunately, the Company cannot respond fully to your request until you give us further details about the information you are seeking. Section 7(3) of the Act states that a data controller must be provided with sufficient information to locate the information which you would like to see. Therefore, to help us respond properly to your request and give you access to the information in which you are most interested, could I ask you to be more specific in your request as follows:

1. You have requested access to all emails, including back-up tapes, which the Company holds about you. To search the Company's entire email system, including back-up tapes, and provide you with copies would involve a disproportionate effort for the Company and we are not therefore willing to provide these copies. I would ask you to be more specific regarding your request for email searches as follows:
   (a) Please can you let us know which period of time you would like us to search against?
   (b) Please provide us with the names of the people whose email accounts you would like us to search. Please note the following points about our policy on email:
   (a) we will only provide copies of emails which are about you as a person and have you as their focus, not every email merely addressed or copied to you or sent by you, which may relate to business activities, rather than you as an individual;

(b) ordinarily, we will only search up to 12 different people's email accounts spanning a 24-month period of your choice. However, if you feel that a wider search would be justified on the basis that it will be necessary to check the accuracy of your data, then please explain your grounds for believing this and we will consider them.

2. I assume that you do not want a copy of information which you have already been given (such as your offer letter, contract of employment and payslips). If this is not the case, please let me know which copies you would like.

[3   Your request for all other documents that mention you is too wide. Such an open-ended request does not meet the requirements of section 7(3) of the Act. Please let me know specifically which documents or type of documents you require, and where it is not obvious, indicate where these documents might be found.]

I look forward to hearing from you.

Yours sincerely

for and on behalf of Bradshaw & Co

Conducting the searches

Request made by: Emma Hollaway
Date compliant request received: 1 March 2004
Deadline for compliance: 9 April 2004
Co-ordinator: Ruth Bradshaw ('RMB')

Source	Search conducted by	Date of search	Date range searched (if applicable)	Search strings used	Documents found	Notes/comments
Brenda Brown's outlook – inbox on server	RMB	2 March 2004	1 January 2003 to 31 January 2004	'Emma Hollaway'; 'EH', 'Emma', 'Ems'	42 emails	Email corrupted from 1 April 2002 – 30 May 2002. Unable to access two password protected documents attached to email 15 August 2003.
Brenda Brown's outlook – sent items on server	RMB	2 March 2004	1 January 2003 to 31 January 2004	'Emma Hollaway', 'EH', 'Emma', 'Ems'	59 emails	
HR Central Storage	LJM	5 March 2004	n/a	n/a	personnel file	Contract of employment not contained within file.
Jack White's employee files	LJM	4 March 2004	n/a	n/a	4 documents	Jack White retains an electronic filing system where he makes informal notes on the employees in his team. HR FOLLOW UP.
Health and Safety central records	LJM	1 April 2004	n/a	n/a	1 document	One accident report recovered.

Sample response to an access request

Ms E Hollaway
42 Cherry Orchard
Appleby
Dorset

Dear Emma

Your access request

Thank you for your letters of 14 February and 1 March 2004 requesting access to the personal data which Bradshaw & Co holds about you under the Data Protection Act 1998.

I enclose a copy of the personal data which we hold and which you have requested. In relation to the enclosed data, please note:

- The purposes for which we have processed and/or currently process the data are for the purposes of your general employment relationship with Bradshaw & Co, as well as any continuing administration of your benefits and the administration of our staff records.
- The recipients or classes of recipient to whom such data is disclosed are other entities in the Bradshaw group of companies and third parties which provide services to Bradshaw & Co.
- The sources of the data are you, other Bradshaw & Co staff and entities in the Bradshaw group of companies and third parties such as service providers and referees.

We have provided all of the information requested in points 1, 3 and 4 of your letter of 1 March 2004.

In relation to point 2 of your letter, we have provided the information requested except some documents which were subject to legal professional privilege which have not been provided.

In relation to point 5 of your letter, we have not provided a copy of the confidential reference which you requested as the data contained in it includes information about a third party who has not consented to its disclosure.

If you have any questions about this letter, or any of the attached documents, please contact me on the number below.

Yours sincerely

for and on behalf of Bradshaw & Co

Sample basic email and internet acceptable use policy

1. Introduction and purpose

The Company recognises that email and the internet are important business tools. The Company's policy is to encourage all workers to develop the skills necessary to use these tools effectively in carrying out their duties. The main reason for providing you with email and internet access is to assist you in effectively carrying out your job.

Why have a policy?

Misuse of the internet or email can expose both you and the Company to legal or financial liability. For example, you may enter into unintended contracts, breach copyright or licensing arrangements, incur liability for defamation or harassment or introduce viruses into the system. This policy is designed to safeguard both you and the Company from such liabilities. It is important that you read it carefully and ensure that any use of the internet or email is in accordance with its terms. The policy sets down guidelines for acceptable use of the Company's computer systems.

Who is covered by the policy?

This policy applies to employees of the Company, workers and other contractors who have access to Company computer systems. It also applies to your personal use of email or the internet where you identify yourself as associated with the Company.

Changes to the policy

The Company may occasionally modify this policy to take account of changes in technology, law and best practice. You will be notified in writing of any change.

2. Guidelines for acceptable use

Email

KEEP IT PROFESSIONAL

Email, just like any other form of communication, should reflect the highest professional standards at all times. You should keep messages brief and to the point, ensure that an appropriate heading is inserted in the subject field and that you check the spelling and grammar before sending. You should also double check the recipient before pressing the send button – not only can it be embarrassing if a message is sent to the wrong person, it can also result in the unintentional disclosure of confidential information about the Company.

The internet is not a secure means of communication and third parties may be able to access or alter messages which have been sent or received. Do not send any information in an email which you would not be happy being publicly available.

PERSONAL USE

Although the primary reason for allowing you access to email is to help you perform your duties more effectively, reasonable personal use of email will be allowed provided that it does not interfere with the performance of your duties.

EMAIL LEAVES RECORDS

Email is a very informal way of communicating, much like speech. Unlike speech however an email leaves a retrievable record. Remember that even when you think you have deleted information it can remain on both your computer and on the Company's back up system. Emails can be recovered as evidence in court proceedings or reviewed by regulators.

WATCH OUT FOR VIRUSES

When using the Company email system be vigilant. Computer viruses are often sent by email and can cause significant damage to the Company's information systems. If you suspect that a file may contain a virus do not open it and contact the IT Department immediately.

Internet

As with email, the internet is provided for your use as a business tool. However, you may make reasonable personal use of the internet provided it does not interfere with your duties.

3. Unacceptable use of email and the internet

As use of the internet and email can give rise to liabilities for both you and the Company, certain activities are prohibited to try to reduce the chances of any such liability arising.

Protecting the system from viruses

You must not open or forward email attachments (particularly executable files) unless they are from a reliable source. You must not download software from the internet or otherwise install unauthorised software on the Company's computer system.

Causing congestion on the system

You must not create congestion on the system by sending unnecessary trivial messages or unnecessary copying or forwarding of messages such as jokes.

Protecting confidentiality

You must not send any confidential information over the internet or by email unless you have the express permission of your line manager.

You must not disclose any of your security passwords to a third party and if you believe that someone else knows your password(s) you must change it.

You must not distribute personal contact details of any employee of the Company without their prior consent.

Complying with the law and best practice

You must not access or send pornographic, offensive, obscene, racist or criminal material or any other material liable to cause embarrassment to the Company or its customers.

You must not act in such a way as to breach copyright or the licensing conditions of any internet site or computer programme.

4. Monitoring

There may be circumstances when the Company requires to access your email or details of your internet use.

General policy

The Company does not as a matter of policy routinely monitor workers' use of the internet or the content of email messages sent or received. However, the Company has a right to protect the security of its systems, check that use of the system is legitimate, investigate suspected wrongful acts and otherwise comply with legal obligations imposed upon it. To achieve these objectives, the Company carries out random spot checks on the system which may include accessing individual email messages or checking on specific internet sites you have accessed.

Other circumstances in which the Company may monitor your email/internet use

In addition, where you are unexpectedly absent from work, or are absent for a prolonged period the Company reserves the right to access your email/details of your internet use to allow it to continue with normal business. Where possible, this will not be done without your prior knowledge.

The Company may also access your emails/monitor your internet use where there are reasonable grounds to suspect you have misused the system either in the scale, content or nature of messages sent. In these circumstances the Company may monitor the destination, source and content of email to or from a particular address and/or use of the internet from a particular terminal.

Personal messages

Except where misuse of the system is suspected, the Company will not open emails the content of which it believes is personal.

Confidentiality

If for any reason the Company does require access to your email or records of your internet use, any information obtained will be treated in the strictest confidence and will not be disclosed to any third party except where necessary.

5. Breach of policy

A breach of this policy may lead to disciplinary action in accordance with the Company's disciplinary policy up to and including dismissal. In addition, or as an alternative, the Company may withdraw your internet or email access.

6. Responsibility

The IT Manager is responsible for the monitoring and implementation of this policy. If you have any questions about the content of this policy or other comments you should contact the IT Manager.

I have read and understood the Company policy on email and internet acceptable use and agree to abide by its terms.

Signed _____

Code of Practice benchmarks for mergers and acquisitions

Part 2, Section 13 Code of Practice

The Code of Practice is not legally binding but represents the Information Commissioner's recommendations to be followed in relation to processing worker data for the purpose of a merger or acquisition.

The benchmarks for disclosure of worker data in mergers and acquisitions

The Code of Practice sets out six benchmarks as follows:
1. Ensure, wherever practicable, that information handed over to another organisation in connection with a prospective acquisition or merger is anonymised.
2. Only hand over personal information prior to the final merger or acquisition decision after securing assurances that:
   (i) it will be used solely for the evaluation of assets and liabilities,
   (ii) it will be treated in confidence and will not be disclosed to other parties, and
   (iii) it will be destroyed or returned after use.
3. Advise workers wherever practicable if their employment records are to be disclosed to another organisation before an acquisition or merger takes place. If the acquisition or merger proceeds, make sure workers are aware of the extent to which their records are to be transferred to the new employer.
4. Ensure that if you intend to disclose sensitive personal data, a sensitive personal data condition is satisfied.
5. Where a merger or acquisition involves a transfer of information about a worker to a country outside the European Economic Area, ensure that there is a proper basis for making the transfer.
6. New employers should ensure that the records they hold as a result of the merger or acquisition do not include excessive information and are accurate and relevant.

Vendor's fair processing notice: due diligence/disclosure

As you know [*Vendor company*] [is in discussions with [*Purchaser company*] about] / [has signed an agreement under which [*Purchaser company*] is to purchase] [*identify potential transaction*]. In order to facilitate the Purchaser's [further] investigations into [*Targetco*], we have established a data-room which will contain information about Targetco's employees.

[**where TUPE applies**] These investigations will also enable the Purchaser to provide us with information about any measures it proposes to take in respect of employees who are affected by the transfer.

We have been asked to provide [outline nature of information to be disclosed in response to the employees' personnel records which may include details of:
- performance appraisals
- disciplinary, grievance and absence records
- career planning records and start date
- gender and marital status
- supervisor
- bank details
- nationality
- home phone number
- salary information and national insurance number.]

[*Note: disclosure of this level of detail may only be appropriate after exchange of contracts*]

[The Purchaser has entered into confidentiality agreements under which it has agreed to:
- restrict disclosure of this data to such of its employees and advisers as are necessary for the purpose of [assessing the potential liabilities and obligations relating to employment matters if the transaction proceeds];
- keep this data secure and to return the data to us if the sale does not proceed within [*specify time frame*].

[**See below if vendor is proceeding with the consent route in order to satisfy the 'fair processing conditions'.** [We request your permission to release this information at [*time/date*]. [**Note: Consent is likely**

to be needed in respect of sensitive personal data] Should any individual wish to withhold this information they should inform [*y*] by email.

[**Asset sale**] On completion, your entire personnel files will transfer to [*Purchaser*] as your new employer. [*Purchaser*] would at that stage be entitled to hold and process any personal data needed (in so far as it is accurate, up-to-date and relevant) for the purposes of the employment relationship.

Please let [*data protection officer / HR officer*] know if you have any queries about this.

Yours faithfully

[*Vendor*]

Purchaser's fair processing notice (asset purchase): on completion

Dear [*name of employee*]

As you know, [*Purchaser*] purchased [*description of business*] on [*effective date of purchase*]. [On that day], your employment transferred to [*Purchaser*] by operation of law [and we have written to you separately about this]. This notice is to advise you of the position in relation to your data protection rights.

Your personnel files and personal data have been transferred to [*Purchaser*] as part of your ongoing employment with [*Purchaser*].

[*Purchaser*] is now going through the process of ensuring that the personal data which it holds in respect of employees is accurate, up-to-date and relevant. [With this in mind, [*Purchaser*] encourages any employee who wants to review the personal data relating to him to do so in order to confirm its accuracy and relevance.]

Please do not hesitate to contact [*Name and position*] on [*telephone/address/email*] if you have any queries.

Yours faithfully

[Purchaser]

Sample purchaser confidentiality undertaking

Purchaser undertakes that:

(a) the information provided [in the data room] and such further information as is provided in response to Purchaser information requests relating to employees of [*Targetco*] (the 'Employee Data') shall be held in confidence;

(b) it shall restrict the disclosure of the Employee Data to such of its employees and advisers as is necessary for the purposes of ascertaining the extent of the potential liabilities and obligations towards such employees]/[identifying employees whose employment will transfer to [   ] under TUPE] and preparing to employ such employees;

(c) it will take adequate measures to protect the security of any personal data having regard to the seventh data protection principle set out in the Data Protection Act 1998;

(d) in the event that the Purchaser does not purchase [*describe target*] within [*set out time frame*] of the provision by the Vendor of the Employee Data, then save as agreed to the contrary, the Employee Data and all copies thereof shall be returned to the Vendor [and/or destroyed by the shredding of paper or the expunging of electronic files];

(e) the Employee Data shall not be disclosed to any other person without the consent of the Vendor, such consent not to be unreasonably withheld. Any such disclosure shall be on terms that the recipient shall enter into a data protection undertaking in like terms. [*This last provision may be particularly relevant in an outsourcing situation where a primary contractor is proposing to sub-contract certain services to sub-contractors who will take on transferring staff*].

Sample discrimination questionnaire consent form

[To be typed on headed notepaper]

[Date]

Strictly private and confidential

Dear [name]

[Sex/race/disability/equal pay act/sexual orientation/religion or belief] Questionnaire — Comparator consent form

[Name of employer] has been served with a Questionnaire under the [specify relevant discrimination legislation] by

_____   (name of complainant) (the "Complainant")

The Complainant believes that [he] [she] may have been [specify alleged discriminatory treatment]. The Complainant considers that this is due to [his] [her] [gender / race / disability / sexual orientation / religion or belief] and [has named you as] [you are] a comparator.

In the Questionnaire, the Complainant has asked us to provide the following details about you

_____   (specify as appropriate).

It is the policy of [name of employer] not to disclose this information in a format from which you can be identified without your consent. You are under no obligation to give your consent to the disclosure of the information.

Sample discrimination questionnaire consent form

If the information is included in the response to the Questionnaire it will be disclosed to [name of employer]'s lawyers, the Complainant and the Complainant's lawyers. It may also be used in employment tribunal proceedings during which any information disclosed may become publicly available.

It is important to remember that the existence and nature of the Questionnaire is a confidential matter and you should not discuss it with any of your colleagues.

If you have any questions please contact me on [telephone number]. Even if you decide to withhold your consent, I should be grateful if you could still take the time to complete the statement below and return the form to me for record keeping purposes. However, unless I hear from you by [insert date in [two] weeks' time], I will assume that you are withholding your consent.

I would like to take this opportunity to thank you in advance for taking the time and the trouble to assist in the above matter.

Please complete the statement below then sign and return a copy of this note to me.

I do/do not* consent to the disclosure and use of my information as outlined above.

*delete as appropriate

Signed _____   Date _____

Please note:

There are certain limited circumstances where [name of employer] may have to provide the information even without your consent, in particular, where there is an order from an employment tribunal compelling [name of employer] to disclose the information or where [name of employer] needs to take legal advice. We would inform you if such a situation arose.

Index

Impact assessments—*contd*
  health information, and—*contd*
    clear purposes, 41
    consideration of legal obligations, 41–42
    introduction, 41
    justification, 42
  workplace monitoring, and
    adverse impact, 72
    alternatives, 72
    clear purposes, 72
    consideration of legal obligations,
      72–73
    introduction, 72
    justification, 73
Inaccurate data, actions against
  generally, 21
**Information concerning employees'
  health**
  See EMPLOYEES' HEALTH INFORMATION
Information made available to public
  exemptions, and, 101–102
Interception of communications
  workplace monitoring, and, 79–80
International data management
  employment records, and, 34
Internet use, monitoring of
  communication, 75
  contents, 73–74
  enforcement, 74–75
  extent of monitoring, 74
  introduction, 73
  purposes, 73–74
  sample, 131–134
Interviews
  recruitment, and, 107
In-vehicle monitoring
  workplace monitoring, and, 76
Iris scanning
  workplace monitoring, and, 68
Isle of Man
  transfer of data overseas, and, 94

Journalism
  exemptions, and, 101
Judicial appointments
  exemptions, and, 102

Lawful purposes
  data protection principles, and, 11–12

'Legal Guidance'
  generally, 2
Legal professional privilege
  exemptions, and, 103
  subject access requests, and, 56
Legitimate interests
  business transfers, 85–86, 86
  discrimination questionnaires, and 111–112
  Schedule 2 condition, and, 14
Limited purposes
  data protection principles, and, 11–12
  employment records, and, 28
  health information, and, 42
Literary purposes
  exemptions, and, 101

Management forecasting
  exemptions, and, 102–103
  subject access requests, and, 55
Manual data
  relevant filing systems, and, 5
Medical examination and testing
  health information, and, 45–46
Monitoring in workplace
  admissibility of evidence, 80
  application of DPA, 68–69
  audio monitoring, 75–76
  business aims, 73
  CCTV monitoring, 76
  Code of Practice
    audio monitoring, 75–76
    CCTV monitoring, 76
    covert monitoring, 76–77
    email monitoring, 73–75
    impact assessments, 72–73
    Internet monitoring, 73–75
    in-vehicle monitoring, 776
    introduction, 71
    policies, 73
    relevant monitoring, 71–72
    security of data, 76
    video monitoring, 75–76
  consent, 77–78
  contractual commitments, 73–74
  covert monitoring, 76–77
  data protection principles, 70–71
  email monitoring
    communication, 75
    contents, 73–74

Voice recognition
workplace monitoring, and, 68

Workplace monitoring
See MONITORING IN WORKPLACE